EASY BOOK OF

ANATOMY

NCBA

MCQ SERIES

EASY BOOK OF ANATOMY

NALINI K. PATHAK

MBBS, MS (Anatomy)

New Central Book Agency (P) Ltd

LONDON

DELHI KOLKATA PUNE HYDERABAD ERNAKULAM

REGD. OFFICE

8/1 Chintamoni Das Lane, Kolkata 700 009, India
email: ncbapvtltd@eth.net

OVERSEAS OFFICE

27 Catherine Court, Chase Road, Southgate, London, N14 4RB

EXPORT OFFICE

212 Shahpur Jat, New Delhi 110 049
email: ncbaexp@ncbapvtltd.com

BRANCHES

4262/3 1st Floor, Flat Nos. 105 & 106
Ansari Road, Daryaganj, New Delhi 110 002
email: ncbadel@ncbapvtltd.com

House No. 3-1-315, 1st Floor
Nimboliadda, Kachiguda, Hyderabad 500 027
email: ncbahydb@ncbapvtltd.com

Shop Nos. 3 & 4, Vinayak Towers
681/B Budhwar Peth, Appa Balwant Chowk
Pune 411 002
email: ncbapune@ncbapvtltd.com

GSS Shopping Complex, 1st Floor
Opposite College Post Office, Convent Road
Ernakulam 682 035
email: ncbaernk@ncbapvtltd.com

EASY BOOK OF ANATOMY

First NCBA Edition: 2008
Reprinted: 2009

PUBLISHER AND TYPESETTER

New Central Book Agency (P) Ltd
8/1 Chintamoni Das Lane, Kolkata 700 009

PRINTER

New Central Book Agency (P) Ltd
Web-Offset Division, Dhulagarh, Sankrail, Howrah

COVER DESIGNER

Prasenjit Halder

COVER PRINTER

Biswanath Studio
3 Garanhatta Street, Kolkata 700 006

TECHNICAL EDITOR

Mita Sen, MBBS

PROJECT TEAM

S Dutta, Suryakanta Chakraborty

ISBN: 81-7381-584-4

Price: Rs 225.00 [Rupees Two Hundred and Twenty-five]

Preface

There is always a voice from my heart to do something for the medical students which makes the anatomy subject very simple and easy for them.

Hence I had tried to make full efforts from my side in this book, so that each and every medical student should always be ready for all the examinations.

This book consist of MCQs and SAQs of anatomy with diagrammatic representation meant for the undergraduate medical students for different medical competitive examinations.

The set of MCQs and SAQs in this book covers all the commonly used formats and all aspects of the subject of anatomy.

This book includes all the modern aspects, concise formats and changing patterns of all the medical competitive examinations carried out throughout the country.

I hope the effort shall prove to be a valuable aid to medical students and help them proceed along the path of success and enable them to face the challenges in anatomy.

Although every care has been taken to ensure the accuracy and to avoid the ambiguity in the wording of questions, the author shall welcome suggestions for improvement.

I wish to express my most sincere and grateful thanks to my colleagues for rendering great help during preparation of this book.

Last but not the least, I extend my heartiest thanks to M/s New Central Book Agency (P) Ltd for taking up the strenuous job of a good publication well in time.

Dr Nalini K Pathak

Professor

Head of Department of Anatomy

NKP Salve Institute of Medical Sciences and Research Centre

Digdoh Hill, Hingana, Nagpur

Recommendation

On perusal of MCQs and SAQs in Anatomy by Prof Dr Mrs N K Pathak, an academic by choice and a teacher par-excellence in the subject of Anatomy. It seems to me, that she has put stupendous effort to prepare it. Anatomy is a vast subject, evidently she has carried out a rigorous and judicious selection of the material so as to cover only essential anatomical facts which are required by a medical student in the exams. She has tried to compile the various aspects of anatomy and systematically presented them in this book in the form of MCQs and SAQs.

Since long time, students were in need of such a book which could bridge the unfortunate hiatus between anatomy and the fresh medical students. This book fills this gap successfully.

This book is most interesting and attractive for its modern aspects. It has freshness and understanding which is derived from the innovative thinking of its author and from his wide and varied experience in teaching anatomy.

The questionnaire are of unusual excellence. They are clear, concise, well-conceived, easily reproducible and are credited to the author.

The appeal of this book should be wide in medical, dental and paramedical fields. I am sure the book will help to broaden the anatomical foundation of the students to make them prudent to face the examinations with confidence and voracity.

I complement and recommend the author for valuable, conceptual leadership, in bringing out such a book, more so as she belongs to the family of NKP Salve Institute of Medical Sciences and Research Centre, Nagpur.

Dean

NKP Salve Institute of Medical Sciences and Research Centre
Digdoh Hill, Hingana, Nagpur

Contents

Chapter 1: General Anatomy

Multiple Choice Questions

1) How many bones are present in human body ?
   a. 120 b. 150
   c. 200 d. 206

2) Shape to the body is given by:
   a. Cartilages b. Muscles
   c. Bones and cartilages d. Bones

3) Abduction movement is:
   a. Towards midline of central axis
   b. Away from midline of central axis
   c. Forward movement
   d. Backward movement

4) Single epiphysis is for:
   a. Metacarpals b. Metatarsals
   c. a + b d. None of the above

5) From primary centre of ossification, the part of the bone formed is:
   a. Metaphysis b. Epiphysis
   c. Diaphysis d. None of the above

Ans. 1. d 2. d 3. b 4. c 5. c

6) Medullary cavity is present in following bones *except*:

a. Humerus b. Radius

c. Femur d. Clavicle

7) Air containing bone is called:

a. Sesamoid bone

b. Pneumatic bone

c. Flat bone

d. Irregular bone

8) Irregular bone is:

a. Single vertebra b. Hip bone

c. a + b d. None of the above

9) Rich blood supply is usually at:

a. Epiphysis b. Diaphysis

c. Metaphysis d. All of the above

10) Bones develop in certain tendons are:

a. Sesamoid bones

b. Short bones

c. Irregular bones

d. Pneumatic bones

11) Following bones are flat bones:

a. Ribs b. Scapula

c. Sternum d. All of the above

Ans. 6. d 7. b 8. c 9. c 10. a 11. d

12) Atavistic epiphysis is for:

a. Head of humerus
b. Coracoid process of scapula
c. Tubercles of humerus
d. Head of metatarsals

13) Free mobility is on:

a. Fibrous joints
b. Primary cartilaginous joints
c. Secondary cartilaginous joints
d. Synovial joints

14) A joint where no movement occurs is:

a. Syndesmosis
b. Symphysis
c. Plane synovial joint
d. All of the above

15) Gomphosis is also called:

a. Ball and socket joint
b. Peg and socket joint
c. Synchondrosis
d. Syndesmosis

16) Rotation movement takes place on:

a. Pivot synovial joint
b. Plane synovial joint
c. Saddle synovial joint
d. Hinge synovial joint

17) Striated muscle is:

a. Smooth muscle
b. Skeletal muscle
c. Both of the above
d. None of the above

Ans. 12. b 13. d 14. a 15. b 16. a 17. b

18) Involuntary but striated muscle is:

a. Cardiac muscle
b. Plane muscle
c. Skeletal muscle
d. None of the above

19) Deltoid muscle is:

a. Unipinnate muscle
b. Bipinnate muscle
c. Multipinnate muscle
d. Flat muscle

20) Walls of the blood vessel receive blood supply from:

a. Surrounding tissue by diffusion method
b. Vasa vasorum
c. Anastomosis
d. None of the above

21) Single layer of Endothelium lines:

a. Arterioles
b. Sinusoids
c. Capillaries
d. Endarteries

22) Retinaculum is:

a. Thick band of superficial fascia
b. Thick band of deep fascia
c. Tendon of the muscle
d. None of the above

23) The part of the muscle which moves is:

a. Origin
b. Insertion
c. Belly
d. None of the above

Ans. 18. a 19. c 20. b 21. c 22. b 23. b

24) Myelin sheath covers:

a. Dendrites
b. Axons
c. Both of the above
d. None of the above

25) Neuroglial cells are as follows *except* :

a. Microglial cells
b. Stellate cells
c. Astrocytes
d. Oligodendrocytes

26) Multipolar cells are in:

a. Spinal root ganglion
b. Sympathetic ganglion
c. Both of the above
d. None of the above

27) Following part of neurone shows Nissl's granules:

a. Cell body
b. Axons
c. Dendrites
d. a + c

28) Spinal root ganglion contains:

a. Pseudounipolar neurones
b. Unipolar neurones
c. Multipolar neurones
d. Bipolar neurones

29) Periosteum shows following features:

a. Has rich nerve supply
b. Sharpeys' fibres connect the periosteum C bone
c. Thick fibrous membrane covers the external surface of bone
d. All of the above

Ans. 24. b 25. b 26. b 27. d 28. a 29. d

30) Cartilage has:

a. No blood vessels
b. No lymphatics
c. No nerves
d. All of the above

31) Articular cartilage is:

a. Hyaline cartilage having perichondrium
b. Hyaline cartilage having no perichondrium covering
c. White fibrocartilage
d. None of the above

32) Rickets is due to:

a. Deficiency of vitamin C
b. Deficiency of vitamin D
c. Lack of collagen fibres
d. Genetic factor

33) Gliding movement is on:

a. Gomphosis
b. Primary cartilaginous joint
c. Plane synovial joint
d. Hinge synovial joint

34) Following statements are true for synovial membrane:

a. Lines the capsule on inside
b. Does not cover the articular part of the bone
c. Secrete synovial fluid which lubricates the joint
d. All of the above

Ans. 30. d 31. b 32. b 33. c 34. d

35) Articular surfaces are reciprocally concavoconvex in:

a. Saddle synovial joint
b. Ellipsoid synovial joint
c. Condyloid synovial joint
d. Pivot synovial joint

36) Following part of the joint has no nerve supply:

a. Capsule of the joint
b. Ligaments of the joint
c. Synovial membrane
d. Articular cartilage covering the articular part of the bone

37) Following tissue is the contractile tissue:

a. Epithelium
b. Connective tissue
c. Muscle tissue
d. Nervous tissue

38) Lanugo is:

a. Foetal skin covered by fine hairs
b. Skin of scalp
c. Eyebrows
d. None of the above

39) Filtering of the lymph is the function of:

a. Tonsils
b. Thymus
c. Lymph node
d. Spleen

40) Filtering of the blood is the function of:

a. Spleen
b. Thymus
c. Both of the above
d. None of the above

Ans. 35. a 36. d 37. c 38. a 39. c 40. a

Short Answer Questions

1) What are the peculiarities of sesamoid bone ?

Ans. 1. These bones develop in the tendon of the muscle

2. Minimise the friction
3. The bone ossifies after birth
4. Has no periosteum
5. Absence of haversian system.

2) Enumerate the arteries which supply the long bone.

Ans. 1. Nutrient artery

2. Epiphyseal arteries
3. Metaphyseal arteries
4. Periosteal arteries.

3) Superficial fascia:

Ans. This is the layer of connective tissue beneath the skin. This contains:

1. Loose areolar tissue
2. Fat
3. Cutaneous blood vessels and nerves
4. Lymphatics.

Modification:

1. Superficial fascia of neck shows Platysma muscle
2. Superficial fascia of pectoral region shows mammary glands
3. In scrotum — muscle in the superficial fascia is Dartos muscle.

Functions:

1. Allows the movement of skin
2. Conserves body heat.

4) Deep fascia and its modification:

Ans. This is also connective tissue, but dense.

It is fibrous sheet having no fat modification of deep fascia.

1. Forms retinacula
2. Forms aponeurosis
3. Forms capsule of the joint
4. Forms bursa
5. In the thigh – deep fascia forms thick band on lateral sides of thigh, and the band is called iliotibial tract
6. Forms carotid sheath –

Tube-like sheath of deep cervical fascia around:

a) Common carotid artery and internal carotid artery
b) Internal jugular vein
c) Vagus nerve.

7. Forms sheath for tendons
8. Forms septa in between the muscles called intermuscular septa.

Functions of deep fascia –

- Fibrous sheet devoid of fat
- Provide surface for attachment of muscles
- Keep the underneath structures in their normal position.

5) Classify cartilaginous joints. Give one example of each.

Ans. 1. Primary cartilaginous joint called synchondrosis.

Cartilage is temporary. It is converted into bone by the process of ossification.

Example, joint between epiphysis and diaphysis of growing bone.

No movement occurs here.

2. Secondary cartilaginous joint called symphysis.

These joints are in midline of body.

Shows slight movements.

Cartilage is permanent — does not ossify.

Example, joint between two vertebrae.

pubic symphysis.

6) Give functions of bones.

Ans. 1. Give the shape to the body by forming skeleton.
2. Give support to the body.
3. Provide surface to the attachment of muscles tendons, capsules and ligaments.
4. Protect certain organs — like brain, spinal cord, lungs, heart, etc.
5. Formation of blood.
6. Store calcium and phosphorus.

7) Define epiphysis. What are the types of epiphysis ? Give examples.

Ans. Epiphysis is the part of the long bone which develops from secondary centre of ossification (i.e. the centre which appears after birth).

Types are –

1. Pressure epiphysis – head of humerus
   head of femur
2. Traction epiphysis – tubercles of humerus
   trochanters of femur
3. Atavistic epiphysis – coracoid process of scapula
4. Aberrant epiphysis – bases of metacarpals and metatarsals
5. Compound epiphysis (i.e. pressure and traction epiphysis).
   Example, ischial tuberosity of hip bone.

8) Name the uniaxial joint with one example of each.

Ans. Hinge joint – allows uniaxial movements,
i.e. flexion + extension.
Example – elbow joint, ankle joint.

Pivot joint – allows rotation.
Example – superior radioulnar joint.
atlantoaxial joint.

9) Classify synovial joints with one example of each.

Ans. 1. Plane synovial joint – allows gliding movements.
Example – sacroiliac joint.

2. Uniaxial joint –

Hinge joint – allows flexion and extension.
Example – elbow joint.

Pivot joint – allows rotation.
Example – superior radioulnar joint.

3. Biaxial joint –

   Ellipsoid – wrist joint.

   Condyloid – temporomandibular joint.

   Movements – flexion
   – extension
   – abduction
   – adduction

4. Multiaxial joint –

   a) Ball and socket – shoulder joint
   – hip joint

   b) Saddle joint – carpometacarpal joint of thumb

   All movements are permitted and allowed.

   Circumduction – combination of all movements.

10) What are the characteristics of synovial joint ?

Ans. 1. Ends of long bone form joint. Ends are covered by articular cartilage called articular ends.

2. Joint is surrounded by capsule. Capsule is lined on inside by synovial membrane. Capsule and synovial membrane is called articular capsule.

3. Joint cavity is present and this potential space allows the movements.

4. Capsule is supplemented by ligaments.

5. Free mobility is observed.

11) What are the different types of bones ?

Ans. As per shape –

1. Long bones
2. Flat bones

3. Short bones
4. Irregular bones
5. Pneumatic bones

As per structure –

1. Cancellous bone or spongy bone. Example, ends
2. Compact bone – shaft bone

As per development –

1. Membranous bone – clavicle
2. Cartilaginous bone – humerus
3. Membrane + Cartilaginous – mandible

Regionwise —

1. Bones of axial skeleton
2. Bones of appendicular skeleton

Sesamoid bones – patella
– fabella
– pisiform

12) Classify the neurones.

Ans. 1. Unipolar – mesencephalic nucleus of trigeminal nerve.
2. Bipolar – neurones in retina.
3. Pseudounipolar – dorsal root ganglion.
4. Multipolar – sympathetic ganglion.

13) Classify fibrous joints.

Ans. These are immovable joints.

1. Sutures in the skull.
2. Gomphosis or peg and socket.
3. Syndesmosis – inferior tibiofibular joint.

14) Name different types of sutural joint.

Ans. 1. Serrate

2. Squamous

3. Plane

4. Denticulate

5. Limbus

15) Metaphysis:

Ans. It is the diaphysis near epiphyseal cartilage.

This is the most vascular area of bone.

Most active area or called zone of active growth.

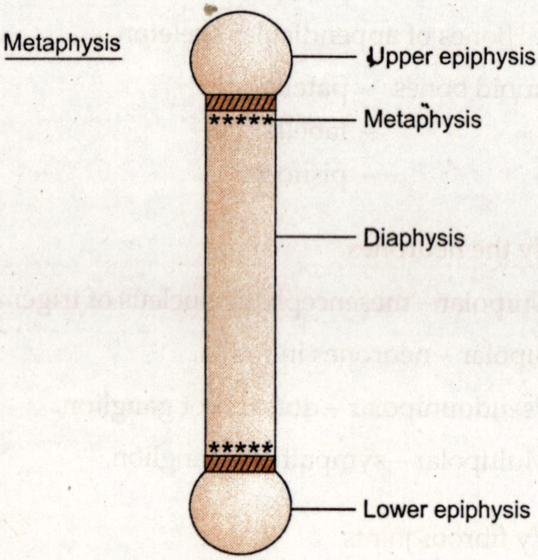

16) Draw and label the diagram of typical synovial joint.

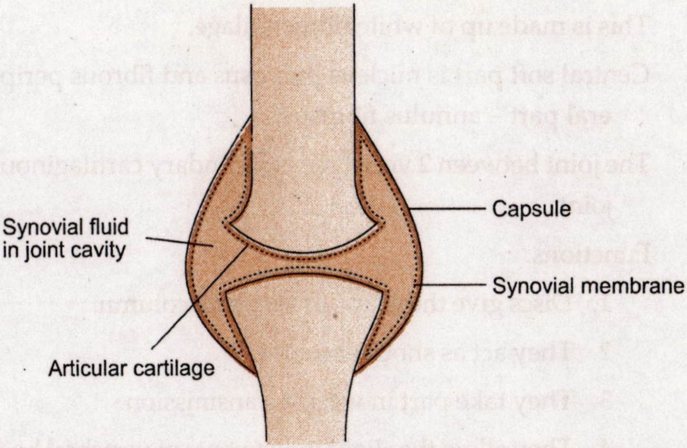

17) Draw the diagram of growing bone and label it.

Ans.

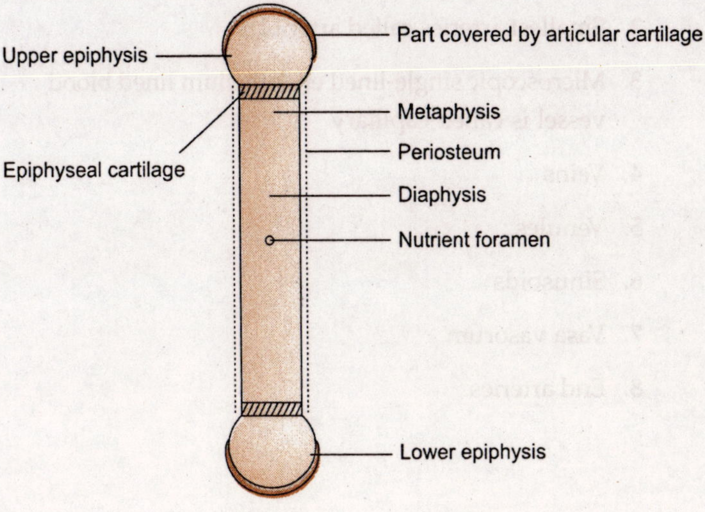

18) Intervertebral disc:

Ans. This lies in between the bodies of two vertebrae.

This is made up of white fibrocartilage.

Central soft part is nucleus pulposus and fibrous peripheral part – annulus fibrosus.

The joint between 2 vertebrae is secondary cartilaginous joint.

Functions:

1. Discs give the shape to vertebral column.
2. They act as shock absorber.
3. They take part in weight transmission.
4. They allow the slight movements of vertebral bodies on each other.

19) What are different types of blood vessels ?

Ans.
1. Arteries
2. Smallest arteries called arterioles
3. Microscopic single-lined endothelium lined blood vessel is called capillary
4. Veins
5. Venules
6. Sinusoids
7. Vasa vasorum
8. End arteries.

20) What are parts of skin ?

Ans. 1. Superficial layer – avascular and ectodermal in origin called epidermis

↓

lined by stratified squamous keratinised epithelium

2. Deeper vascular layer – fibrous is dermis

↓

Mesodermal in origin

21) Give the different functions of skin.

Ans. 1. Skin gives protection to underlying tissue.

2. Absorbs – exterior ointment if applied to skin, it is absorbed.

3. Prevents water loss from the body.

4. The pigment present in the epidermis. This pigment is called melanin. Pigment protect the tissues against harmful effects of light, specially ultraviolet light.

5. Protect the tissue from damage by heat.

6. Skin is very important sensory organ.

7. Skin regulates the body temperature.

In warm climate cooling of the body is by sweating.

22) What are the appendages of skin ?

Ans. 1. Hairs – skin is almost covered by hair except palm, sole

2. Nails

3. Sebaceous glands

4. Sweat glands.

23) Periosteum:

Ans. This is thick fibrous covering the external surface of the bone. It is tightly adherent to bone.

The periosteum shows:

a. Outer fibrous layer

b. Inner cellular layer

↓

which is osteogenic

Periosteum is united to underlying bone by Sharpey's fibres.

There are periosteal arteries which nourish the bone.

Periosteum has rich nerve supply. The periosteum is the most sensitive part of the bone.

24) Movements of synovial joints:

Ans. 1. Gliding movements

2. Angular movements
   - Flexion
   - Extension
   - Abduction
   - Adduction
3. Rotation
4. Circumduction.

25) Explain Hilton's Law.

Ans. This law states that motor nerve to the muscle acting on the joint gives a branch to the capsule of the same joint and another branch supplies the skin covering the joint.

Chapter 2: Histology

General Histology: Multiple Choice Questions

1) Rough endoplasmic reticulum is necessary for synthesis of:

   a. Carbohydrates   b. Proteins

   c. Fat   d. None of the above

2) Lysosomes of cytoplasm are responsible for:

   a. Phagocytosis   b. Synthesis

   c. Absorption   d. None of the above

3) Barr body is:

   a. Cell organelle   b. Pigment

   c. Chromosome   d. Foreign body

4) An epithelium which is multilayered is called:

   a. Simple   b. Stratified

   c. Pseudostratified   d. None of the above

5) Basement membrane is made of:

   a. Epithelial tissue   b. Connective tissue

   c. Muscular tissue   d. None of the above

6) Secreting part of cycloplasm is:

   a. Golgi bodies   b. Nucleus

   c. Rough endoplasmic reticulum

   d. Smooth endoplasmic reticulum

Ans. 1. b 2. a 3. c 4. b 5. b 6.a

7) Cells having height more and width less is known as:

a. Columnar cells
b. Cuboidal cells
c. Squamous cells
d. None of the above

8) Acrosomal cap contains:

a. Mitochondria
b. Golgi apparatus
c. Rough endoplasmic reticulum
d. Smooth endoplasmic reticulum

9) Hair-like processes on top of cell moving in one direction only are:

a. Cilia
b. Stereocilia
c. Microvilli
d. Tail of the spermatozoa

10) Following statements are true *except*:

a. Group of cells to perform the different functions are called tissues
b. Muscle cell is having contractile power
c. Nissl's granules of neurone are rough endoplasmic reticulum
d. Bone absorbing cells are called osteoblasts

11) An epithelium which appears multilayered but is truely single layer of cells called as:

a. Simple epithelium
b. Stratified epithelium
c. Pseudostratified epithelium
d. None of the above

Ans. 7.a 8.b 9.a 10.d 11. c

12) Following are examples of simple epithelium *except*:

a. Skin

b. Uterine tube

c. Alveoli of lung

d. Thyroid follicles

13) Example of ciliated columnar epithelium is:

a. Uterine tubes b. Large intestine

c. Small intestine d. Oesophagus

14) Epithelium which shows cells having height and width same is:

a. Simple squamous epithelium

b. Simple cuboidal epithelium

c. Simple columnar epithelium

d. None of the above

15) Pseudostratified ciliated epithelium is seen in:

a. Small intestine b. Urethra

c. Ureter d. Trachea

16) Transitional epithelium is found in following organs *except*:

a. Ureters

b. Urinary bladder

c. Collecting ducts of kidney

d. Some parts of urethra

Ans. 12. a 13. a 14. b 15. d 16. c

17) Exocrine gland in which entire cell goes in the secretion is:

a. Holocrine in nature b. Apocrine in nature

c. Merocrine in nature d. None of the above

18) Which of the following statements is correct ?

a. Sebaceous gland is holocrine

b. Transitional epithelium lines kidney

c. Nucleus of serous cell is flat and on base

d. Lung alveoli are lined by stratified epithelium

19) Loose connective tissue shows following cells *except*:

a. Fibroblasts b. Plasma cells

c. Lymphocytes d. Chondrocytes

20) Following structure belongs to regularly arranged dense tissue:

a. Tendon

b. Interosseus membrane

c. Deep fascia

d. Superficial fascia

21) Superficial fascia is example of:

a. Loose connective tissue

b. Dense regular connective tissue

c. Specialised connective tissue

d. None of the above

Ans. 17. a 18. a 19. d 20. a 21. a

22) Signet ring appearance of cell is in:

a. Pigment cell
b. Plasma cell
c. Fat cell
d. Mast cell

23) Fibroblast cell produces:

a. Collagen fibres
b. Elastic fibres
c. Reticular fibres
d. All of the above

24) Following fibres does not branch:

a. Collagen fibres
b. Elastic fibres
c. Reticular fibres
d. None of the above

25) Capsule of the joint is example of:

a. Specialised connective tissue
b. Dense connective tissue
c. Loose connective tissue
d. None of the above

26) Following cartilage is not present in human being:

a. Hyaline cartilage
b. Fibrocartilage
c. Cellular cartilage
d. Elastic cartilage

Ans. 22. c 23. d 24. b 25. b 26. c

27) In which cartilage matrix is homogenous ?

a. Hyaline cartilage
b. Cellular cartilage
c. Elastic cartilage
d. White fibrocartilage

28) Following are hyaline cartilages *except*:

a. Epiglottis
b. Trachea
c. Cricoid cartilage
d. Epiphyseal cartilage

29) Osteon is the structural unit of:

a. Muscle
b. Cartilage
c. Bone, i.e. compact bone
d. Membrane

30) Following cell is multinuclear cell:

a. RBCs
b. Lymphocytes
c. Osteoclasts
d. Osteoblasts

31) Osteoblasts carry the process of:

a. Bone formation
b. Bone absorption
c. Both of the above
d. None of the above

32) Striated muscle fibre is:

a. Multinucleate cell
b. Mononucleate cell
c. No nucleus
d. None of the above

Ans. 27. a 28. a 29. c 30. c 31. a 32. a

33) Sarcomere is the part of myofibril situated between two:

a. Two Z bands

b. Two M bands

c. Two H bands

d. None of the above

34) Muscle coat of hollow viscera is of:

a. Nonstriated smooth muscle fibres

b. Cardiac muscle fibres

c. Striated muscle fibres

d. None of the above

35) Cardiac muscle fibres shows all characters *except*:

a. Presence of intercalated discs

b. Single nucleus in the cell

c. Faint striations

d. Multiple nuclei along cell wall

36) Myoepithelial cells are showing following features:

a. Ectodermal in origin

b. Contractile cell

c. No striation

d. All of the above

37) Nissl's granules are present in:

a. Osteocytes b. Myocytes

c. Neurones d. Chondrocytes

Ans. 33. a 34. a 35. d 36. d 37. c

38) Nissl's granules are:

a. Rough endoplasmic reticulum

b. Smooth endoplasmic reticulum

c. Golgi apparatus

d. Phagocytes

39) Nissl's granules are not present in which part of neurone:

a. Cell body
b. Dendrites
c. Axons
d. None of the above

40) Microglial cells are helping in:

a. Synthesis

b. Support

c. Phagocytosis

d. Myelination of nerve fibres

41) Aorta is the example of:

a. Elastic artery
b. Muscular artery
c. End artery
d. None of the above

42) Following arteries are muscular arteries:

a. Umbilical arteries

b. Radial arteries

c. Femoral arteries

d. All of the above

Ans. 38. a 39. c 40. c 41. a 42. d

43) Following glands are ectodermal *except*:

a. Mammary glands
b. Pituitary gland
c. Sweat glands
d. Liver

44) Following gland is mesodermal:

a. Suprarenal cortex
b. Sebaceous gland
c. Interstitial cells of Leydig of testes
d. a + c

45) Following are white fibrocartilages:

a. Labrum acetabulum
b. Labrum glenoidale
c. Menisci of knee joint
d. Intervertebral disc
e. All of the above

46) Following glands are endodermal:

a. Liver
b. Pancreas
c. Thyroid
d. All of the above

47) Microscopic blood vessel is called:

a. Arteries
b. Capillaries
c. Venules
d. None of the above

Ans. 43. d 44. d 45. e 46. d 47. b

48) Cartilage of ear is:

a. White fibrocartilage
b. Yellow elastic cartilage
c. Hyaline cartilage
d. Cellular cartilage

49) Following statements are correct, *except*:

a. Arteries have thick media
b. Cartilage in the wall of trachea is hyaline
c. Striated muscle fibre shows branching
d. Fat-cell shows signet ring appearance

50) Single layer of endothelium is in:

a. Arterioles
b. Capillaries
c. Sinusoids
d. End arteries

51) Arteries shows:

a. Thick tunica intima
b. Thick tunica media
c. Thick tunica adventitia
d. None of the above

52) Subcapsular lymph sinus is in:

a. Lymph node
b. Tonsils
c. Spleen
d. Thymus

Ans. 48. b 49. c 50. b 51. b 52. a

53) Hassall's corpuscles are in:

a. Tonsils
b. Thymus
c. Spleen
d. None of the above

54) Cilia are present in:

a. Uterine tubes
b. Trachea
c. Bronchus
d. All of the above

55) Which layer of epidermis is well-formed in non-hairy thick skin:

a. Stratum spinosum
b. Stratum granulosum
c. Stratum lucidum
d. Stratum corneum

56) Goblet cell is:

a. Unicellular serous secreting gland
b. Unicellular mucus secreting gland
c. The secretion goes to blood
d. Multicellular gland

57) Argentaffin fibres are:

a. Reticular fibres
b. Collagen fibres
c. Elastic fibres
d. None of the above

58) Which type of lymphocytes are produced by thymus ?

a. B lymphocytes
b. T lymphocytes
c. Both of the above
d. None of the above

Ans. 53. b 54. d 55. c 56. b 57. a 58. b

59) Typical sweat gland is:

a. Simple tubular gland
b. Simple coiled tubular gland
c. Simple alveolar
d. Compound tubular gland

60) Following statement is *not* correct:

a. Sweat glands are exocrine
b. Endocrines have ducts
c. Mammary glands are modified sweat glands
d. Cells with microvilli are seen in small intestine

61) Blood supply of large blood vessels is by:

a. Capillaries b. Arterioles
c. Vasa vasorum d. Sinusoids

62) There are no muscle tissue in the wall of:

a. Arteries b. Arterioles
c. Veins d. Sinusoids

63) Cristae are in:

a. Endoplasmic reticulum
b. Golgi apparatus
c. Mitochondria
d. None of the above

Ans: 59. b 60. b 61. c 62. d 63. c

Systemic Histology: Multiple Choice Questions

1) Tracheal cartilages are:
   a. Hyaline cartilage
   b. Elastic cartilage
   c. Fibrocartilage
   d. None of the above

2) Pulmonary surfactant is produced by:
   a. Type I cells
   b. Type II cells
   c. Type III cells
   d. None of the above

3) Substance of tongue is formed by:
   a. Skeletal muscle
   b. Smooth muscle
   c. Fibrous tissue
   d. Elastic cartilage

4) Lingual tonsils are in:
   a. Anterior 2/3 of tongue
   b. Posterior 1/3 of tongue
   c. Whole of tongue
   d. Sides of tongue

5) Growth hormone is secreted by:
   a. Corticotrophs
   b. Somatotrophs
   c. Mammotrophs
   d. Gonadotrophs

Ans. 1. a 2. b 3. a 4. b 5. b

6) Oxytocin is released by:

a. Pars anterior
b. Pars intermedius
c. Pars posterior
d. Pars tuberalis

7) Thyrocalcitonin is secreted by:

a. Follicular cells of thyroid gland
b. Parafollicular cells of thyroid gland
c. Chief cells of parathyroid gland
d. None of the above

8) Parathormone is produced by:

a. Chief cells
b. Oxyphil cells
c. Both of the above
d. None of the above

9) Cornea has:

a. Rich blood supply
b. Poor lymphatics
c. Rich nerve supply
d. None of the above

10) Following is vascular coat of eyeball:

a. Sclera
b. Cornea
c. Retina
d. Choroid

11) Optic nerve fibres are axons of:

a. Ganglion cells
b. Bipolar cells
c. Rods and cones
d. None of the above

Ans. 6. c 7. b 8. a 9. c 10. d 11. a

12) Pigment cells of retina are:

a. Squamous cells
b. Cuboidal cells
c. Columnar cells
d. Polyhedral cells

13) Which cells of retina respond to bright light:

a. Rod cells
b. Cone cells
c. Both of the above
d. None of the above

14) Lacrimal gland is:

a. Serous gland
b. Mucus gland
c. Seromucus gland
d. None of the above

15) Supporting tissue of mammary gland is:

a. Fibrous
b. Fatty
c. Fibrofatty
d. Fibromuscular

16) Folds of stomach are called as:

a. Rugae
b. Villi
c. Crypts
d. Valves of Kerkring

17) Pepsin is secreted by:

a. Oxyntic cells
b. Chief cells
c. Mucus neck cells
d. Agrentaffin cells

Ans. 12. b 13. b 14. a 15. c 16. a 17. b

18) Villi are in:

a. Large intestine
b. Stomach
c. Small intestine
d. None of the above

19) Brunner's glands are in submucosa of:

a. Stomach
b. Duodenum
c. Small intestine
d. Large intestine

20) Taenia coli is the feature of:

a. Large intestine
b. Small intestine
c. Stomach
d. Duodenum

21) Central vein of hepatic lobule opens in:

a. Portal vein
b. Hepatic vein
c. Portal and hepatic vein
d. None of the above

22) Portal triad contains following structures *except*:

a. Portal vein
b. Hepatic artery
c. Hepatic vein
d. Bile duct

23) Pancreas is:

a. Exocrine gland
b. Endocrine gland
c. a + b
d. Mucus gland

Ans. 18. c 19. b 20. a 21. b 22. c 23. c

24) Islets of Langerhans are in:

a. Spleen b. Liver

c. Pancreas d. Suprarenal gland

25) Proximal convoluted tubules of kidney are lined by:

a. Cuboidal cells with brush border

b. Cuboidal cells without brush border

c. Squamous cells

d. Columnar cells

26) Juxtaglomerular cells are modified cells in the walls of:

a. Afferent arteriole

b. Efferent arteriole

c. Proximal convoluted tubule

d. Distal convoluted tubule

27) Which enzyme is liberated by juxtaglomerular cells ?

a. Renin b. Angiotensin I

c. Angiotensin II d. None

28) Seminiferous tubules of testes show following cells *except*:

a. Spermatogonia b. Spermatocytes

c. Cells of Leydig d. Sertoli cells

29) Spermiogenesis is:

a. Spermatogonia to primary spermatocytes

b. Spermatocytes to spermatid

c. Spermatids to spermatozoa

d. None of the above

Ans. 24. c 25. a 26. a 27. a 28. c 29. c

30) Corpora amylacea is seen in:

a. Kidneys b. Prostate
c. Spleen d. Liver

31) Supportive tissue of prostate is:

a. Fibrous b. Fibrofatty
c. Fibromuscular d. None of the above

32) Corpus luteum of ovary secretes:

a. Oestrogen b. Progesterone
c. Both of the above d. None of the above

33) Uterine tubes are lined by:

a. Simple columnar epithelium
b. Simple cuboidal with microvilli
c. Simple columnar with cilia
d. Stratified columnar

34) Glands of uterus show screw-like appearance in:

a. Resting phase b. Proliferative phase
c. Secretory phase d. None of the above

35) Cortisone is produced by:

a. Zona glomerulosa
b. Zona fasciculata
c. Zona reticularis
d. None of the above

Ans. 30. b 31. c 32. b 33. c 34. c 35. b

36) Following hormone is secreted by adrenal medulla:

a. Mineralocorticoids

b. Glucocorticoids

c. Androgens

d. Adrenalin

37) Purkinje cells are characteristic of:

a. Cerebrum

b. Cerebellum

c. Dorsal root ganglion

d. None of the above

38) Betz cells are in:

a. Cerebrum

b. Cerebellum

c. Ventral horn cells of spinal cord

d. Dorsal horn cells of spinal cord

Ans. 36. d 37. b 38. a

Short Answer Questions

1. Give histology of cardiac MS fibre.

Ans.

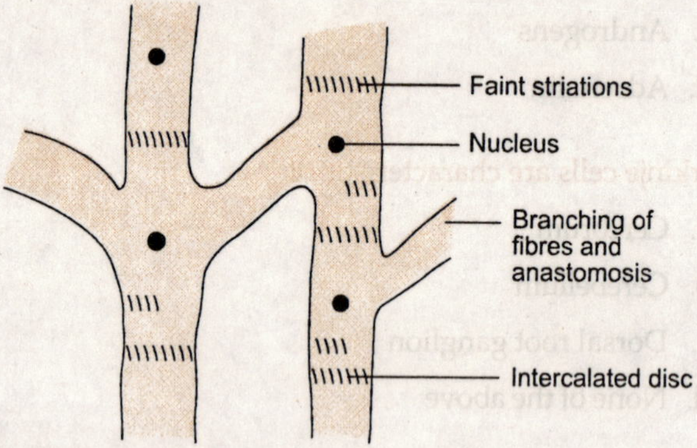

Cardiac muscle fibre is mononucleate.

Shows branching and anastomosis.

Junction between two adjacent cells – dark line seen called intercalated disc.

2. Give histology of thymus.

Ans.

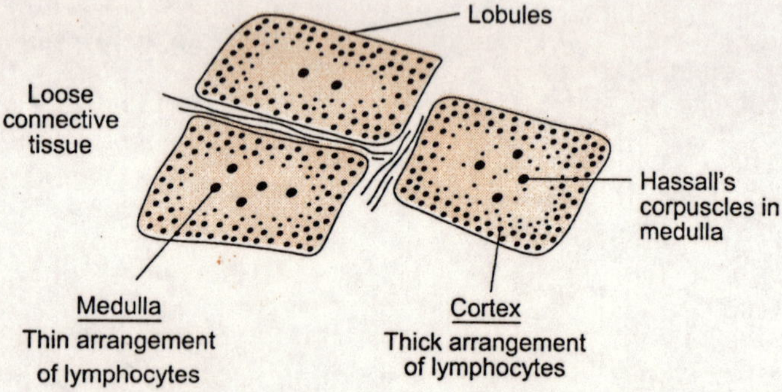

Shows lobules.

Outer zone is cortex – thicker arrangement of lymphocytes.

Inner zone – the medulla shows thinner arrangement of lymphocytes

+

Characteristic feature of thymus.

In medulla – Hassall's corpuscles seen.

3. Give the histology of tonsil.

Ans.

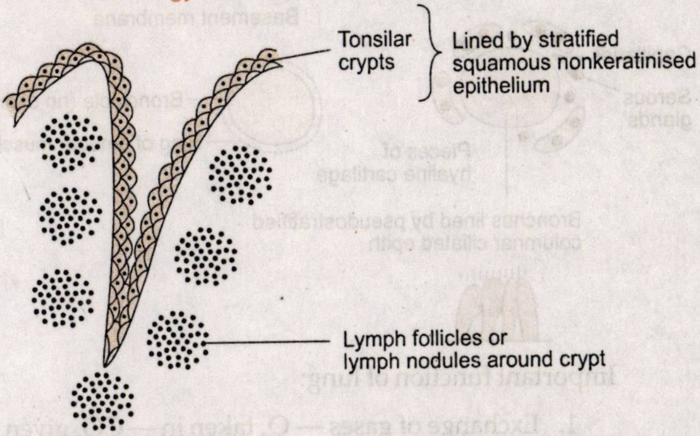

- Shows tonsillar crypts lined by stratified squamous moist variety.
- Around the crypts — rounded groups of lymphocytes called lymph follicles.

Details of lymph follicle

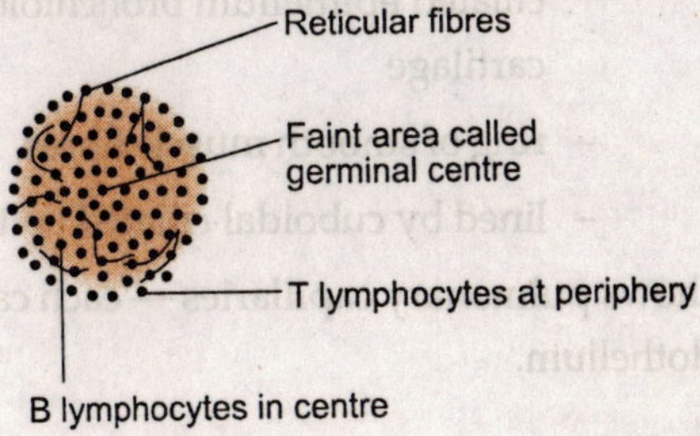

4. **Give the histology of lung.**

Ans.

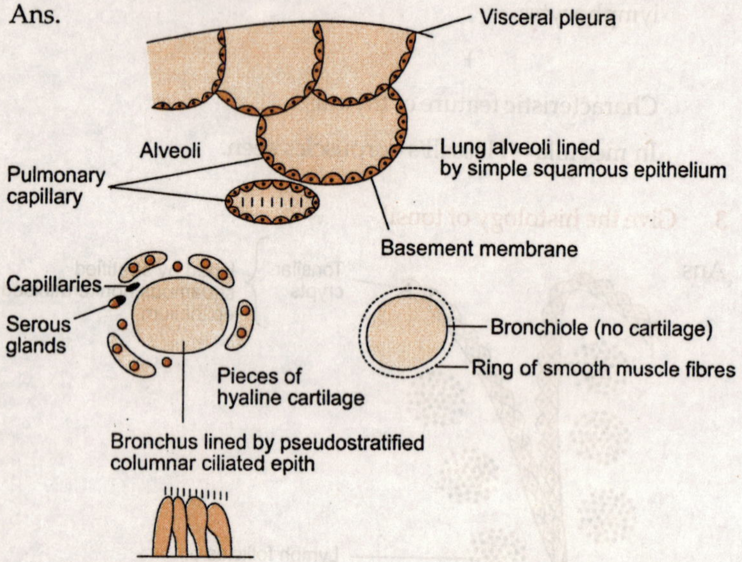

Important function of lung:

1. Exchange of gases — O_2 taken in — CO_2 given out
2. Oxygenation of blood.

Slide shows multiple thin-walled air spaces called lung alveoli.

Bronchus – pieces of hyaline cartilage

– lined by pseudostratified columnar ciliated epithelium bronchioles — no cartilage

– ring of smooth muscle fibres

– lined by cuboidal ciliated epithelium

Also shows pulmonary capillaries — each capillary is lined by endothelium.

5. Name the different neurones in cerebellum.

Ans. 1. Purkinje cells.

Flask-shaped cells arranged in single layer with regular interval.

Long axon arises from base of flask.

Purkinje cells in cerebellum

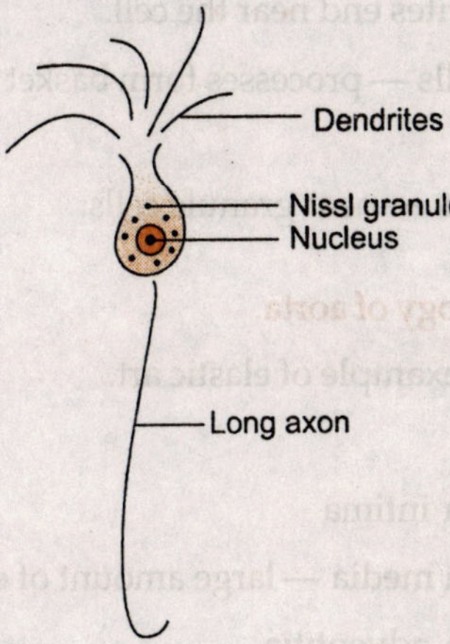

2. Granule cells.

Small cell large nucleus.

4-5 dendrites.

Axon goes up and divides in T-shaped manner.

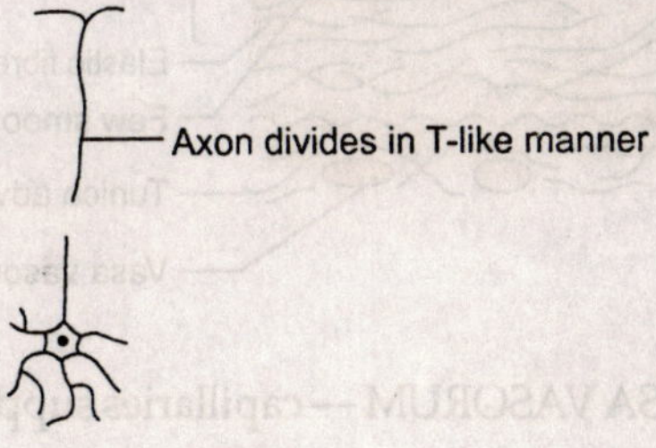

3. Stellate cells — star-shaped.

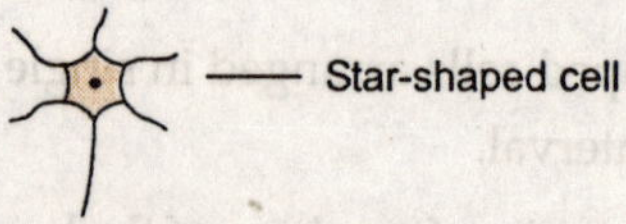

Cell has very short Axon.

4-5 dendrites end near the cell.

4. Basket cells — processes form basket around Purkinje cells.

5. Golgi cells — near granule cells.

6. Give the histology of aorta.

Ans. Aorta is the example of elastic art.

Got 3 coats:

1. Tunica intima
2. Tunica media — large amount of elastic fibres
3. Tunica adventitia

Note: VASA VASORUM — capillaries supply walls of aorta.

7. Give the histology of submandibular salivary gland.

Ans. Seromucus in nature shows serous and mucus acini.

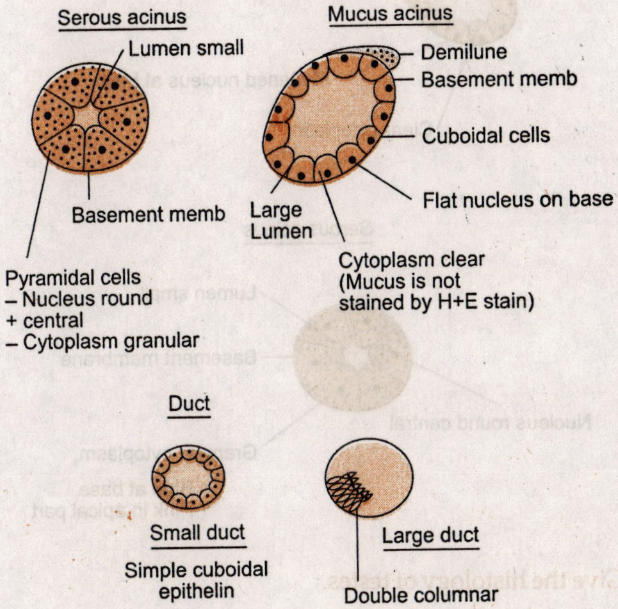

8. Give the difference between serous acinus and mucus acinus.

Ans.

Serous acini round lined by basement membrane, cells lining are pyramidal, cells nucleus round, cytoplasm granular due to granules serous acini darkly stained	Mucus acini oval, round, pear-shaped, lined by basement membrane, cells lining are cuboidal cytoplasm foamy nucleus – flat and on the base
Serous cell in electron microscope	Mucus cell

Mucus acinus

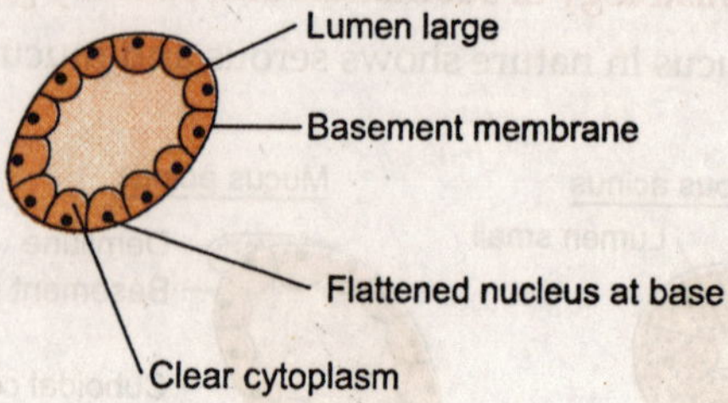

Serous acinus

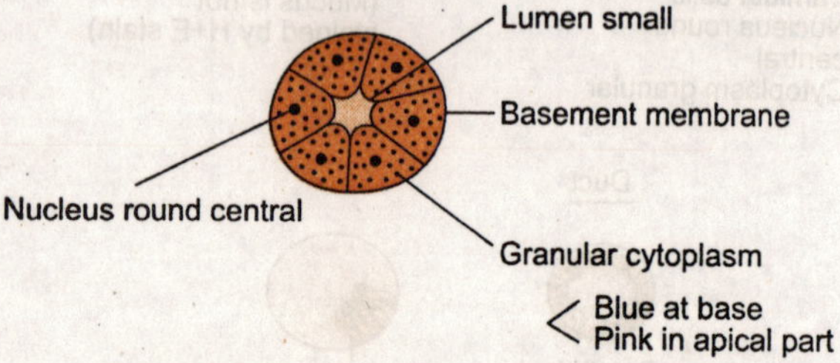

9. Give the histology of testes.

Ans.

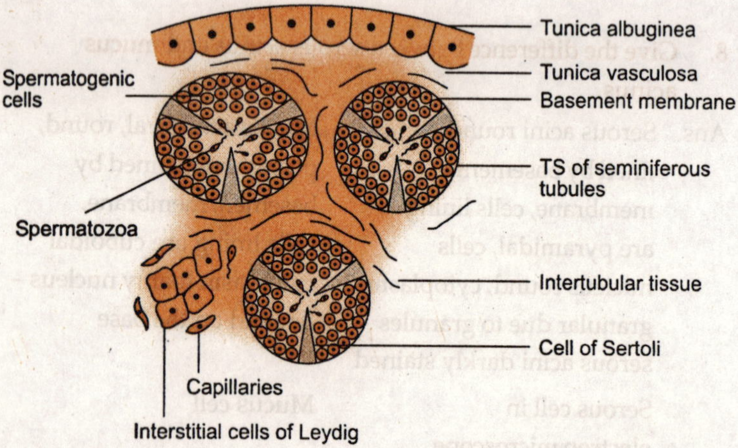

The testes shows covering of

a. Tunica albuginea
b. Tunica vasculosa

T.S. of seminiferous tubules:

Each tubule is lined by basement membrane.

Inside tubule — 2 types of cells seen

a. Spermatogenic cells
b. Cells of Sertoli — called also nursing cells.

Cells of Sertoli provides

a. Nutrition to spermatozoa
b. Mechanical support to spermatozoa
c. Help in phagocytosis
d. Provides fluid medium in which spermatozoa moves.

In between seminiferous tubules — polyhedral cells in groups. They show lipid pigments called interstitial cells of Leydig. These cells secrete testosterone. The cells are surrounded by rich capillaries carrying testasterone.

There are 2 functions of testes:

a. Spermatogenesis
b. Secretion of testosterone — goes to blood

This is endocrine secretion of testes.

10. Give histology of ovary.

Ans.

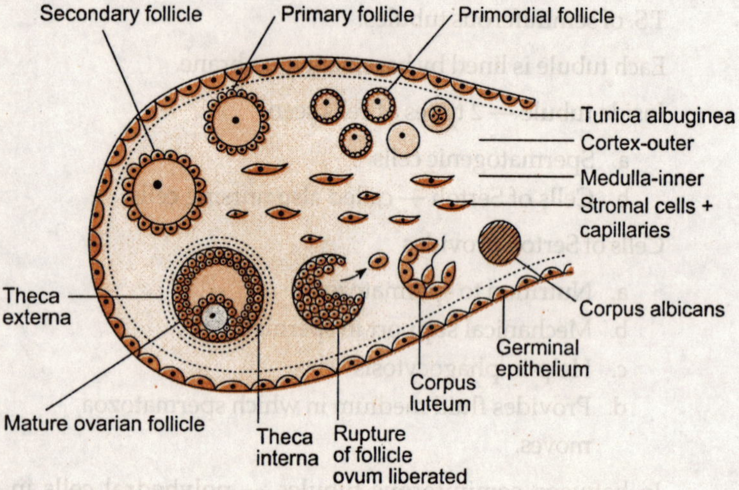

Ovaries – 2 functions:

a. Formation of ovum

b. Theca interna secretes oestrogen

c. Corpus luteum secretes progesterone

Ovaries are covered by germinal epithelium which is simple cuboidal.

Under the germinal epithelium lies tunica albuginea.

Outer part — cortex — shows various stages in the development of ovarian follicles.

Inner part — medulla shows stromal cells + blood vessels.

Chapter 3: General Embryology

Multiple Choice Questions

1) At which cell stage the embryo is called morula ?

a. Four cell stage b. Sixteen cell stage

c. Eight cell stage d. Twelve cell stage

2) Zona pellucida disappears at:

a. Fertilisation of ovum

b. Two cell stage of embryo

c. When embryo occupies the lumen of uterus

d. None of the above

3) Which of the following layers is formed first ?

a. Ectoderm b. Mesoderm

c. Endoderm d. All of the above

4) One primary spermatocyte give rise to how many spermatozoa ?

a. Four b. Two

c. One d. Eight

5) Origin of notochord is:

a. Ectodermal b. Endodermal

c. Mesodermal d. a + c

Ans. 1. b 2. c 3. c 4. a 5. a

6) **Ectoderm forms following structures *except*:**

a. Anterior pituitary gland b. Mammary gland

c. Neutral tube d. Thyroid

7) **Somites are formed by:**

a. Mesonephric duct

b. Paraxial mesoderm

c. Intermediate cell mass

d. Lateral plate of secondary mesoderms

8) **Primary villus of placenta is made up of:**

a. Syncytiotrophoblasts and cytotrophoblasts

b. Syncytiotrophoblasts, cytotrophoblasts, extraembryonic mesoderm

c. Syncytiotrophoblasts, cytotrophoblast, extraembryonic mesoderm and foetal blood vessel

d. None of the above

9) **When the blood vessel appears in the chorionic villus of placenta, then the villus is:**

a. Tertiary villus b. Primary villus

c. Secondary villus d. None of the above

10) **Human placenta is:**

a. Haemoendothelial b. Haemochoreal

c. Epitheliochoreal d. Endotheliochoreal

Ans. 6. d 7. b 8. a 9. a 10. b

11) Epithelium of ureter is derived from:

a. Mesoderm

b. Endoderm

c. Ectoderm and mesoderm

d. Ectoderm

12) Following are mesodermal structure *except*:

a. Adrenal cortex

b. Spleen

c. Sweat glands of skin

d. Kidneys

13) Following statements are true for metaphysis:

a. Highly vascular

b. Give attachment to the muscles

c. Marrow cavity is absent

d. All of the above

14) Somites form following *except*:

a. Sclerotome b. Neurotome

c. Dermatome d. Myotome

15) Occipital myotomes form:

a. Muscles of soft palate

b. Muscles of tongue

c. Muscles of eyeball

d. Muscles of upper limb

Ans. 11. a 12. c 13. d 14. b 15. b

16) Following parts of skin are ectodermal *except*:

a. Epidermis
b. Sweat glands
c. Sebaceous glands
d. Dermis

17) Remains of notochord is:

a. Nucleus pulposus of intervertebral disc
b. Periphery of the intervertebral disc
c. Both of the above
d. None of the above

18) Supporting cells of spermatogenesis are:

a. Interstitial cells of Leydig
b. Sertoli cells
c. Spermatids
d. Secondary spermatocyte

19) During spermatogenesis, first meiotic division is at the level of:

a. Spermatogonia to primary spermatocyte
b. Primary spermatocyte to secondary spermatocyte
c. Spermatid to spermatozoa
d. None of the above

20) Following statement is *not* correct:

a. Spermatid to spermatozoa is spermiogenesis
b. Corpus luteum forms progesterone
c. Leydig cells secrete oestrogen
d. Sertoli cells are supporting cells

Ans. 16. d 17. a 18. b 19. b 20. c

21) Acrosomal cap shows:

a. Mitochondria

b. Rough endoplasmic reticulum

c. Nucleus

d. Golgi apparatus

22) Oestrogen is secreted by:

a. Ovarian follicles   b. Theca externa cells

c. Theca interna cells   d. Corpus luteum

23) After ovulation, ovum reaches the uterine cavity by:

a. Third day   b. Fourth day

c. Ten weeks   d. Four weeks

24) Implantation in human beings is:

a. Central   b. Eccentric

c. Interstitial   d. Any of the above

25) Preoccipital somites give rise to:

a. Muscles of eye

b. Muscles of neck

c. Muscles of upper limb

d. Muscles of tongue

26) Preoccipital somites are supplied by:

a. Oculomotor nerve   b. Trochlear nerve

c. Abducent nerve   d. All of the above

Ans. 21. d 22. c 23. b 24. a 25. a 26. d

27) Neural crest cells form:

a. Epidermis of skin
b. Notochord
c. Pigment cells of skin
d. Dermis of skin

28) Nail is modified part of:

a. Stratum basale of epidermis
b. Stratum spinosum
c. Stratum corneum
d. Stratum lucidum

29) Cells forming enamel of teeth are:

a. Odontoblasts
b. Ameloblasts
c. Melanoblasts
d. Cementocytes

30) Odontoblasts give rise to:

a. Pulp
b. Enamel
c. Dentine
d. None of the above

31) Foregut derivatives are as follows *except*:

a. Oesophagus
b. Stomach
c. First half of duodenum
d. Ileum

32) First organ of body start functioning is:

a. Heart
b. Spleen
c. Liver
d. Central nervous system

Ans. 27. c 28. d 29. b 30. c 31. d 32. a

Short Answer Questions

1. What are abnormal sites of implantation ?

Ans. a. Fallopian tube

b. Ovary

c. Abdominal cavity

2. Which is normal place of implantation ?
In human beings, what type of implantation takes place ?

Ans. Normal site of implantation is posterior wall of uterus at the junction of fundus and body.

In human beings — there is interstitial implantation.

3. Enumerate the functions of placenta.

Ans. 1. Protection

2. Respiration

3. Nutrition

4. Excretion

5. Hormone production

4. What are foetal membranes ?

Ans.
- Chorion
- Amnion
- Yolk sac
- Allantois

5. What are the stages of spermatogenesis ?

Ans. Spermatogonia

↓ Mitosis

Primary spermatocyte

↓ 1st meiotic division

Secondary spermatocyte

↓ 2nd meiotic division

Spermatids

↓ Spermiogenesis

Spermatozoa

6. Name the derivatives of neural crest.

Ans. 1. Spinal ganglion
2. Autonomic nervous system ganglion
3. Schwann cells
4. Pia mater
5. Arachnoid mater
6. Pigment cells in the skin
7. Suprarenal medulla

7. Name the derivatives of neural tube.

Ans. 1. Central nervous system
2. Retina
3. Pineal body
4. Posterior pituitary gland

8. Derivatives of foregut are:

Ans. 1. Oral cavity

2. Pharynx
3. Tongue
4. Tonsils
5. Respiratory system
6. Stomach
7. Duodenum — proximal 1/2
8. Liver, biliary apparatus, pancreas

9. Derivatives of midgut are:

Ans. 1. Distal half of duodenum

2. Jejunum
3. Ileum
4. Caecum
5. Appendix
6. Ascending colon
7. Right 2/3 of transverse colon

10. Derivatives of hindgut are:

Ans. 1. Left 1/3 of transverse colon

2. Descending colon
3. Sigmoid colon
4. Rectum
5. Upper 2/3 of anal canal
6. Urinary bladder
7. Most of urethra

Chapter 4: Superior Extremity

Multiple Choice Questions

1) Clavicle has following peculiarities *except*:
   a. The long bone lies horizontally
   b. Develops in the cartilage
   c. The bone has no medullary cavity
   d. First bone to ossify

2) Following bone is the flat bone:
   a. Sacrum
   b. Patella
   c. Scapula
   d. Maxilla

3) Following is the example of atavistic epiphysis:
   a. Acromion of scapula
   b. Head of humerus
   c. Lesser tubercle of humerus
   d. Coracoid process of scapula

4) Extent of scapula is from:
   a. First rib to sixth rib
   b. Second rib to seventh rib
   c. First rib to fifth rib
   d. None of the above

Ans. 1. b 2. c 3. d 4. b

5) Surgical neck of humerus is related to:

a. Radial nerve

b. Axillary nerve

c. Posterior circumflex humeral artery

d. b + c

6) Bicipital groove of humerus lodges the tendon of:

a. Short head of Biceps b. Long head of Biceps

c. Both of the above d. None of the above

7) Latissimus dorsi is inserted in:

a. Floor of bicipital groove

b. Lateral margin of bicipital groove

c. Back of greater tubercle of humerus

d. Medical margin of bicipital groove

8) Following is not the member of rotator cuff:

a. Teres minor b. Pectoralis minor

c. Subscapularis d. Supraspinatus

9) Tip of the coracoid process gives attachment to:

a. Long head of Triceps

b. Short head of Biceps

c. Short head of Biceps and Coracobrachialis

d. Brachioradialis

Ans. 5. d 6. b 7. a 8. b 9. c

10) Spiral groove of humerus lodges:

a. Profunda brachii artery b. Radial nerve

c. a + b d. Ulnar nerve

11) Biceps brachii is inserted on:

a. Anterior part of radial tuberosity

b. Posterior part of radial tuberosity

c. Ulnar tuberosity

d. Deltoid tuberosity

12) Following are true for Deltoid *except*:

a. Example of multipennate muscle

b. Supplied by axillary nerve

c. Gives rounded appearance to shoulder

d. Does 0 – 20 degree abduction of shoulder joint

13) The nerve behind medical epicondyle of humerus is:

a. Ulnar nerve

b. Median nerve

c. Musculocutaneous nerve

d. Radial nerve

14) The musculocutaneous nerve pierces:

a. Brachialis muscle

b. Coracobrachialis muscle

c. Biceps brachii muscle

d. Brachioradialis muscle

Ans. 10. c 11. b 12. d 13. a 14. b

15) Brachialis is supplied by:

a. Median nerve
b. Musculocutaneous nerve
c. Radial nerve
d. b + c

16) Radial collateral artery arises from:

a. Radial artery
b. Profunda brachii artery
c. Brachial artery
d. None of the above

17) Supraspinatus muscle is doing:

a. 0 – 20 degree abduction of shoulder joint
b. 20 – 90 degree abduction of shoulder joint
c. Above head abduction
d. None of the above

18) Suprascapular nerve arises from:

a. Lower trunk of brachial plexus
b. Roots of brachial plexus — C 4, 5, 6
c. Branches of posterior cord
d. Upper trunk

19) Suprascapular artery arises from:

a. 1st part of axillary artery
b. 2nd part of axillary artery
c. 3rd part of axillary artery
d. Subclavian artery

Ans. 15. d 16. b 17. a 18. d 19. d

20) Through suprascapular foramen passes:

a. Suprascapular artery
b. Suprascapular nerve
c. Suprascapular vein
d. None of the above

21) Pectoralis major muscle is supplied by:

a. Medial pectoral nerve
b. Lateral pectoral nerve
c. a + b
d. None of the above

22) Pectoralis minor moves scapula:

a. Forwards
b. Upwards
c. Downwards
d. Forwards and downwards

23) Pectoralis minor is pierced by:

a. Lateral pectoral nerve
b. Nerve to Subclavius
c. Medial pectoral nerve
d. a + b

24) Following muscle is not in anterior wall of axilla:

a. Pectoralis major b. Teres major
c. Pectoralis minor d. Subclavius

Ans. 20. b 21. c 22. d 23. c 24. b

25) Acromioclavicular joint is:

a. Fibrous joint

b. Primary cartilaginous joint

c. Plane synovial joint

d. None of the above

26) Sternoclavicular joint is:

a. Saddle synovial joint

b. Plane synovial joint

c. Secondary cartilaginous joint

d. Hinge synovial joint

27) Nerve to Subclavius has root value of:

a. C 5, 6 b. C 5, 6, 7

c. C 8, T 1 d. C 7, 8

28) Serratus anterior has following truths *except*:

a. Form posterior boundary of axilla

b. Supplied by long thoracic nerve

c. Originating from upper eight ribs

d. Its paralysis causes winging of scapula

29) Clavipectoral fascia is pierced by:

a. Lateral pectoral nerve

b. Thoracoacromial artery

c. Cephalic vein

d. All of the above

Ans: 25. c 26. a 27. a 28. a 29. d

30) Mammary glands are situated in:
a. Deep fascia of pectoral region
b. Superficial fascia of pectoral region
c. Pectoralis major
d. None of the above

31) Ligaments of Cooper is the feature of:
a. Liver
b. Kidney
c. Mammary glands
d. Skin

32) Axillary lymph nodes drain:
a. Upper outer quadrant of breast
b. Lower outer quadrant of breast
c. Lower and medial quadrant of breast
d. a + b

33) Supporting part of mammary gland is:
a. Fibrous tissue
b. Fibrous and muscular tissue
c. Fibrous and fatty tissue
d. Fat

34) Tubercles of Montgomery are described as:
a. Modified sweat glands
b. Modified sebaceous glands
c. Serous glands
d. None of the above

Ans. 30. b 31. c 32. d 33. c 34. b

35) Long thoracic nerve arises from:

a. Roots of brachial plexus C 5, 6, 7

b. From upper trunk of brachial plexus

c. From posterior cord of brachial plexus

d. From lateral cord of brachial plexus

36) Teres major muscle shows following facts *except*:

a. Member of rotator cuff

b. Supplied by lower subscapular nerve

c. Form post-wall of axilla

d. Inserted on medial lip of bicipital groove

37) Axillary nerve supplies:

a. Deltoid muscle

b. Teres minor muscle

c. a + b

d. Teres major

38) Following muscle is multipennate:

a. Pectoralis major b. Latissimus dorsi

c. Deltoid d. Teres major

39) Flattening of shoulder is due to injury to:

a. Axillary nerve

b. Radial nerve

c. Suprascapular nerve

d. None of the above

Ans. 35.a 36. a 37. c 38. c 39. a

40) Nerve to Serratus anterior has roots:

a. C 4, 5, 6
b. C 5, 6, 7
c. C 5, 6
d. C 8, T 1

41) Winging of scapula is result of injury to:

a. Dorsal scapular nerve
b. Suprascapular nerve
c. Long thoracic nerve
d. None of the above

42) Following muscle has no attachment to scapula:

a. Pectoralis major
b. Pectoralis minor
c. Teres major
d. Teres minor

43) Erb's point is the point of formation of:

a. Upper trunk
b. Middle trunk
c. Lower trunk
d. None of the above

44) Suprascapular nerve supplies:

a. Supraspinatus muscle
b. Infraspinatus muscle
c. Scapula
d. All of the above

45) The contents of cubital fossa are as follows *except*:

a. Median nerve
b. Ulnar nerve
c. Tendon of Biceps brachii
d. Brachial artery

Ans. 40. b 41. c 42. a 43. a 44. d 45. b

46) Medial boundary of cubital fossa is by:

a. Brachioradialis

b. Coracobrachialis

c. Pronator teres

d. Pronator quadratus

47) Median nerve has following facts *except*:

a. Enters forearm in between two heads of Pronator teres

b. Called farmer's nerve

c. Supplies Flexor digitorum superficialis

d. Supplies Flexor carpi ulnaris

48) Following is hinge synovial joint:

a. Shoulder joint b. Wrist joint

c. Elbow joint d. Superior radioulnar joint

49) Head of radius is surrounded by:

a. Radial collateral ligament

b. Capsule

c. Annular or ring ligament

d. None of the above

50) Supination and pronation movements are on:

a. Superior radioulnar joint

b. Inferior radioulnar joint

c. Middle radioulnar joint

d. a + b

Ans. 46. c 47. d 48. c 49. c 50. d

51) In flexed elbow the muscle which helps in supination of forearm is:

a. Brachioradialis
b. Supinator
c. Biceps brachii
d. Brachialis

52) Example of pivot joint is:

a. Superior radioulnar joint
b. Wrist joint
c. Both of the above
d. None of the above

53) Median nerve gives following branch:

a. Medial cutaneous nerve of forearm
b. Medial pectoral nerve
c. Anterior interosseous nerve
d. Posterior interosseous nerve

54) Pronator teres has following facts *except*:

a. Form medial boundary of cubital fossa
b. Supplied by ulnar nerve
c. Got humeral and ulnar head
d. Supplied by median nerve

55) Radial nerve supplies following muscles *except*:

a. Brachialis
b. Anconeus
c. Brachioradialis
d. Extensor carpi ulnaris

Ans. 51. c 52. a 53. c 54. b 55. d

56) **Supinator muscle is pierced by:**

a. Radial nerve

b. Posterior interosseous nerve

c. Anterior interosseous nerve

d. None of the above

57) **Following bones form wrist joint *except*:**

a. Head of ulna

b. Lower end of radius

c. Scaphoid

d. Lunate

58) **Ellipsoid synovial joint is:**

a. Inferior radioulnar joint

b. Wrist joint

c. Carpometacarpal joint of thumb

d. Metacarpophalangeal joint

59) **Radial nerve is injured in:**

a. Saturday night paralysis

b. Crutch palsy

c. Wrist drop

d. All of the above

60) **Deep to flexor retinaculum lies following structures *except*:**

a. Median nerve

b. Ulnar nerve and ulnar artery

c. Four tendons of Flexor digitorum superficialis

d. Four tendons of Flexor digitorum profundus

Ans. 56. b 57. a 58. b 59. d 60. b

61) Flexor retinaculum is:

a. Superficial fascia
b. Deep fascia
c. Aponeurosis of the muscle
d. Tendon of Palmaris longus

62) Carpometacarpal joint of thumb is:

a. Synovial-pivot variety
b. Synovial-condyloid variety
c. Synovial-saddle variety
d. None of the above

63) For head of humerus:

a. Pressure epiphysis b. Traction epiphysis
c. Atavistic epiphysis d. Aberrant epiphysis

64) Glenoid cavity of scapula is directed:

a. Forwards
b. Downwards
c. Forwards and laterally
d. Backwards

65) Glenoidal labrum consists of:

a. Hyaline cartilage
b. White fibrocartilage
c. Yellow elastic cartilage
d. None of the above

Ans. 61. b 62. c 63. a 64. c 65. b

66) Supraglenoid tubercle gives attachment to:

a. Origin of short head of Biceps

b. Origin of long head of Triceps

c. Origin of Coracobrachialis

d. Origin of long head of Biceps

67) Triceps brachii muscle shows following facts *except*:

a. Has long head, lateral head and medial head

b. Supplied by radial nerve

c. Flexor of elbow

d. Inserted on olecranon process of ulna

68) Thumb movements are affected due to injury to:

a. Ulnar nerve b. Median nerve

c. Both of the above d. None of the above

69) Palmar aponeurosis is:

a. Tendon of Palmaris brevis

b. Tendon of Flexor carpi radialis longus

c. Tendon of Palmaris longus

d. All of the above

70) All the muscles of hypothenar eminence are supplied by:

a. Superficial branch of ulnar nerve

b. Deep branch of ulnar nerve

c. Deep branch of median nerve

d. Ulnar and median nerve

Ans. 66. d 67. c 68. b 69. c 70. b

71) Palmaris brevis is supplied by:

a. Superficial branch of ulnar nerve

b. Deep branch of ulnar nerve

c. Superficial branch of median nerve

d. None of the above

72) Inability to oppose the thumb with little finger is due to paralysis of:

a. Opponens digiti minimi brevis

b. Opponens pollicis brevis

c. Flexor pollicis brevis

d. None of the above

73) Klumpke's paralysis is injury to:

a. Upper trunk of brachial plexus

b. Middle trunk of brachial plexus

c. Lower trunk of brachial plexus

d. Ulnar nerve

74) Graveyard of deep branch of ulnar nerve is:

a. Abductor pollicis brevis b. Adductor pollicis

c. Palmaris brevis d. None of the above

75) All the muscles of thenar eminence are supplied by:

a. Ulnar nerve b. Median nerve

c. Radial nerve d. None of the above

Ans. 71. a 72. b 73. c 74. b 75. b

76) **Origin of lumbricals is from:**

a. Four tendons of Flexor digitorum superficialis

b. Four tendons of Flexor digitorum profundus

c. Extensor digitorum tendons

d. None of the above

77) **Flexor carpi ulnaris has:**

a. Insertion on pisiform bone

b. Flexor of wrist

c. Supplied by ulnar nerve

d. All of the above

78) **Loss of initiation of abduction of shoulder joint is injury to:**

a. Subscapular nerve

b. Axillary nerve

c. Suprascapular nerve

d. None of the above

79) **Ulnar nerve is having root value of:**

a. C 6, 7, 8 b. C 8, T 1

c. C 7, 8 d. C 6, 7, 8, T 1

80) **First lumbrical muscle is supplied by:**

a. Median nerve

b. Ulnar nerve

c. Both of the above

d. None of the above

Ans. 76. b 77. d 78. c 79. b 80. a

81) Fourth lumbrical muscle is supplied by:

a. Ulnar nerve – deep branch

b. Median nerve

c. Ulnar nerve – superficial branch

d. Ulnar and median nerve

82) Number of Interossei muscles in hand is:

a. Six b. Seven

c. Eight d. Four

83) Fingers are abducted by:

a. Palmar interossei muscles

b. Lumbricals

c. Dorsal interossei

d. Abductor hallucis brevis

84) Dorsal digital expansion gives insertion to following muscles *except*:

a. Extensor digitorum b. Extensor indicis

c. Interossei d. Lumbricals

85) Following muscles are flexors of wrist *except*:

a. Flexor carpi radialis

b. Flexor carpi ulnaris

c. Palmaris longus

d. Brachioradialis

Ans. 81. a 82. c 83. c 84. b 85. d

86) Following muscles are having double nerve supply *except*:

a. Pectoralis major
b. Subscapularis
c. Brachialis
d. Pronator teres

87) Weakness of flexion of elbow is injury to:

a. Median nerves
b. Ulnar nerves
c. Musculocutaneous nerves
d. None of the above

88) Most medial structure in cubital fossa is:

a. Brachial artery
b. Tendon of biceps
c. Radial nerve
d. Median nerve

89) Deformity in Klumpke's paralysis is:

a. Wrist drop
b. Claw hand
c. Policeman's tip
d. Flat shoulder

90) Following nerves are in contact with humerus *except*:

a. Axillary nerve
b. Radial nerve
c. Ulnar nerve
d. Median nerve

91) Segments of spinal cord involved in Klumpke's paralysis is:

a. C 8, T 1
b. C 5, 6
c. C 7
d. C 5, 6, 7

Ans. 86. d 87. c 88. d 89. b 90. d 91. a

92) The nerve usually compressed in carpal tunnel syndrome is:

a. Ulnar nerve
b. Radial nerve
c. Median nerve
d. Median and ulnar nerves

93) Truths of the movements of supination and pronation are as follows *except*:

a. They take place on superior and inferior radioulnar joints
b. Pronation movement is powerful
c. Powerful supinator in flexed elbow is Biceps brachii
d. Supinator is weak supinator and pierced by posterior interosseous nerve

94) Colles fracture is the fracture of:

a. Lower end of ulna
b. Shaft of humerus
c. Lower end of radius
d. Scaphoid bone

95) Fingers of hand are adducted and abducted on:

a. Interphalangeal joints
b. Metacarpophalangeal joints
c. Carpometacarpal joints
d. None of the above

Ans. 92. c 93. b 94. c 95. b

96) Median nerve supplies following structures *except*:

a. Nail-bed of thumb

b. Muscles of thenar eminence

c. Fourth lumbrical muscle

d. Palmaris longus

97) Following are the contents of axilla *except*:

a. Brachial plexus

b. Brachial artery

c. Axillary artery and its branches

d. Axillary vein

98) Axillary sheath for axillary vessels is derived from:

a. Clavipectoral fascia

b. Pectoral fascia

c. Prevertebral layer of cervical fascia

d. None of the above

99) Skin over tip of shoulder is supplied by:

a. Phrenic nerve b. Supraclavicular nerve

c. Axillary nerve d. Lateral pectoral nerve

100) Following muscles are abductors of shoulder *except*:

a. Supraspinatus

b. Deltoid

c. Serratus anterior and Trapezius

d. Infraspinatus

Ans. 96. c 97. b 98. c 99. b 100. d

101) Axillary nerve supplies following *except*:

a. Skin over upper part of Deltoid
b. Skin over lower part of Deltoid
c. Teres minor muscle
d. Shoulder joint

102) Winging of scapula is injury to:

a. Subscapular nerve
b. Long thoracic nerve
c. Suprascapular nerve
d. Dorsal scapular nerve

103) Proximal row of carpal bones show following bones *except*:

a. Scaphoid
b. Lunate
c. Hamate
d. Triquetral

104) Strongest ligament attached to clavicle is:

a. Interclavicular ligament
b. Sternoclavicular ligament
c. Costoclavicular ligament
d. Coracoclavicular ligament

105) Apex of axilla is bounded by following parts *except*:

a. First rib
b. Upper border of scapula
c. Clavicle
d. Suprasternal notch

Ans. 101. a 102. b 103. c 104. d 105. d

106) Following muscles are supplied by branches of brachial plexus *except*:

a. Pectoralis major

b. Serratus anterior

c. Latissimus dorsi

d. Trapezius

107) Radial nerve is called as the continuation of:

a. Posterior cord of brachial plexus

b. Lateral cord of brachial plexus

c. Medial cord of brachial plexus

d. None of the above

108) Radial nerve supplies long head of Triceps when it is in:

a. Spiral groove of humerus

b. Axilla

c. Anterior compartment of arm

d. Front of lateral epicondyle of humerus

109) Following bone is the membrane bone:

a. Humerus b. Scapula

c. Clavicle d. Ulna

110) Greater tubercle of humerus provides insertion to following muscles *except*:

a. Supraspinatus b. Subscapularis

c. Infraspinatus d. Teres minor

Ans. 106. d 107. a 108. b 109. c 110. b

111) Suprascapular artery has following points *except:*

a. Passes above suprascapular ligament

b. Branch of axillary artery

c. Anastomosis around scapula

d. Branch of subclavian artery

112) Produnda brachii artery has following points *except:*

a. Lies in spiral groove of humerus

b. Branch of brachial artery

c. Forms anastomosis around elbow

d. Gives a branch called radial recurrent artery

113) Anconeus muscle is supplied by:

a. Posterior interosseous nerve b. Radial nerve

c. Ulnar nerve d. None of the above

114) Posterior wall of axilla is formed by following muscles *except:*

a. Latissimus dorsi b. Teres major

c. Teres minor d. Subscapularis

115) Palmar interossei are:

a. Four in number and adduct the fingers

b. Unipennate muscles

c. Supplied by deep branch of ulnar nerve

d. All of the above

Ans. 111. b 112. d 113. b 114. c 115. d

116) Dorsal interossei are:

a. Bipennate muscles

b. Abductors of fingers

c. Supplied by deep branch of ulnar nerve

d. All of the above

117) Thumb is supplied by:

a. Princeps pollicis artery b. Radial artery

c. Ulnar artery d. None of the above

118) Long head of Triceps arises from:

a. Tip of the coracoid process

b. Supraglenoid tubercle

c. Infraglenoid tubercle

d. Acromion of scapula

119) Capsular ligament of shoulder joint is attached to:

a. Surgical neck of humerus

b. Anatomical neck of humerus

c. Morphological neck of humerus

d. None of the above

120) Triceps brachii is inserted on:

a. Coronoid process of ulna

b. Coracoid process of scapula

c. Olecranon process of ulna

d. None of the above

Ans. 116. d 117. a 118. c 119. b 120. c

121) In the proximal row of carpal bones the sequence is:

a. Scaphoid, lunate, triquetral and pisiform

b. Lunate, scaphoid, triquetral and pisiform

c. Scaphoid, lunate, pisiform and triquetral

d. Scaphoid, hamate, lunate and pisiform

122) Most commonly cephalic vein drain into:

a. External jugular vein b. Basilic vein

c. Axillary vein d. Subclavian vein

123) Which vein of superior limb is selected for intravenous injection:

a. Basilic vein b. Axillary vein

c. Cephalic vein d. Median cubital vein

124) Peaud'orange appearance of skin over mammary gland is seen in:

a. Carcinoma breast b. Abscess in breast

c. During lactation d. When lactation is over

125) Nerve of Bell or long thoracic nerve supplies:

a. Pectoralis major b. Pectoralis minor

c. Latissimus dorsi d. Serratus anterior

126) Axillary artery continues as:

a. Brachial artery b. Subclavian artery

c. Radial artery d. None of the above

Ans. 121. a 122. c 123. d 124. a 125. d 126. a

127) Following artery is not the branch of brachial artery:

a. Profunda brachii b. Radial collateral
c. Ulnar collateral d. Radial recurrent

128) Superficial flexors of forearm are supplied by median nerve *except*:

a. Palmaris longus
b. Flexor carpi radialis longus
c. Flexor carpi ulnaris
d. Flexor digitorum superficialis

129) Following structures lie deep to the flexor retinaculum *except*:

a. Ulnar nerve
b. Median nerve
c. Tendon of Flexor digitorum superficialis
d. Tendons of Flexor digitorum profundus

130) Skin of little finger is supplied by:

a. Median nerve b. Radial nerve
c. Ulnar nerve d. Median and ulnar nerve

131) The nerve injured in wrist-drop is:

a. Axillary b. Radial
c. Ulnar d. Median

132) Axillary vein is continuation of:

a. Basilic vein b. Subclavian vein
c. Cephalic vein d. None of the above

Ans. 127. d 128. c 129. a 130. c 131. b 132. a

133) Following muscle is supplied by axillary nerve:

a. Teres major b. Teres minor
c. Pectoralis major d. Pectoralis minor

134) Accessory nerve supplies:

a. Trapezius b. Deltoid
c. Latissimus dorsi d. None of the above

135) Through quadrangular space passes:

a. Axillary nerve
b. Posterior circumflex humoral artery
c. a + b
d. Anterior circumflex humeral artery

136) Interphalangeal joints are:

a. Plane synovial
b. Hinge synovial
c. Condyloid synovial
d. None of the above

137) Nerves are thickened in:

a. Malignancy b. Leprosy
c. Viral diseases d. None of the above

138) Whitlow is the infection of:

a. Adductor space b. Lumbrical spaces
c. Pulp space d. Midpalmar space

Ans. 133. b 134. a 135. c 136. b 137. b 138. c

Short Answer Questions

1. Enumerate the different groups of axillary lymph nodes and its applied aspect.

Ans. 5 groups – Anterior or pectoral
– Posterior or subscapular
– Lateral
– Apical
– Central – lies in fat of axilla

Applied – These glands drain the pectoral region including the mammary glands (breasts) so in carcinoma in breast, these glands get swollen due to metastasis

Treatment – Along with breast tissue, the axillary lymph nodes of same side as well as opposite side are removed.

2. Enumerate the branches of posterior cord of brachial plexus.

Ans. 1. Upper subscapular
2. Lower subscapular
3. Nerve to Latissimus dorsi or thoracodorsal nerve
4. Radial nerve
5. Axillary nerve

3. What is Erb's point ? What is Erb's paralysis ? Name the condition in Erb's paralysis.

Ans. Formation of upper trunk is by the union of C 5, C 6.

Point of formation of upper trunk is Erb's point.

Injury to upper trunk is Erb's paralysis.

Condition of upper limb is policeman's tip.

4. Clavipectoral fascia:

Ans. This is the fascia which lies between

- Clavicle and Subclavius above
- Pectoralis minor below.

The fascia is described as deep fascia.

This is pierced by:

1. Cephalic vein
2. Thoracoacromial artery
3. Lateral pectoral nerve
4. Lymph vessels from base of breast.

Diagram

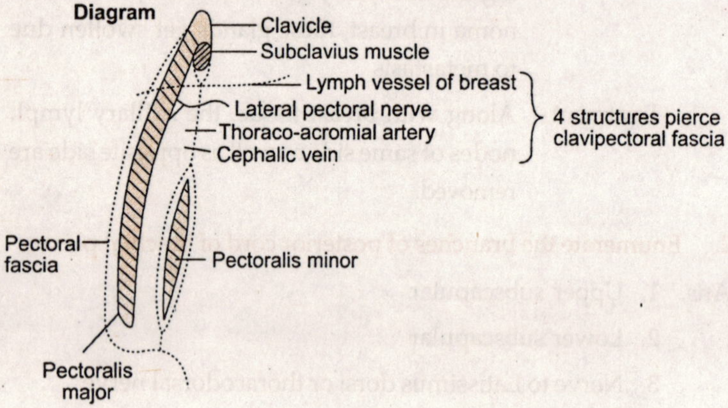

5. Enumerate the branches of axillary artery.

Ans. 1st part — gives one branch, i.e. superior thoracic artery.

2nd part — gives two branches:

1. Thoracoacromial artery
2. Lateral thoracic artery

3rd part — gives three branches:

1. Subscapular artery
2. Anterior circumflex humeral artery

3. Post-circumflex humeral artery

Total six branches.

6. Winging of scapula:

Ans. This condition is because of injury to nerve to Serratus anterior or long thoracic nerve.

Only muscle supplied by this nerve is Serratus anterior gets paralysed.

When the person does the action of this muscle, i.e. over head abduction — scapula becomes prominent from back — look like wings, hence called winging of scapula.

7. Suprascapular nerve:

Ans. Arises from upper trunk of brachial plexus C 5, 6 – are roots.

Supplies – 2 (muscle) – Supraspinatus
– Infraspinatus
2 (joints) – Acromioclavicular joint
– Shoulder joint ends by supplying scapula.

Passes through suprascapular foramen.

8. Intermuscular spaces:

Ans. Upper triangular space — transmits circumflex scapular artery.

Lower triangular space — radial nerve
— profunda brachii artery

Quadrangular space

1. Axillary nerve
2. Posterior circumflex humoral artery

7

9. Name the joints on which Biceps brachii act. What is the action ?

Ans. 1. On shoulder joint – Short head of Biceps flexes shoulder joint
– Long head of Biceps stabilises head of humerus in glenoid cavity

On elbow joint – Flexion of elbow

On superior radioulnar joint – Powerful supinator of forearm

10. Arteries forming anastomosis around scapula:

Ans. 1. Circumflex scapular artery

↓

Branch of subscapular artery – from 3rd part of axillary artery

2. Suprascapular artery of subclavian artery
3. Transverse cervical of subclavian artery

11. Contents of cubital fossa and boundaries of cubital fossa.

Ans. Triangular depression in front of elbow is cubital fossa.

Medially – Pronator teres

Laterally – Brachioradialis

Base – The imaginary line connecting lateral epicondyle of humerus and medial epicondyle of humerus

Floor – Brachialis muscle
Supinator muscle

Roof – Bicipital aponeurosis

Contents:

1. Median cubital vein is on the bicipital aponeurosis
2. Tendon of Brachii muscle
3. Brachial artery
4. Median nerve
5. Radial nerve
6. Two branches of brachial artery

Radial – smaller

Ulnar – larger

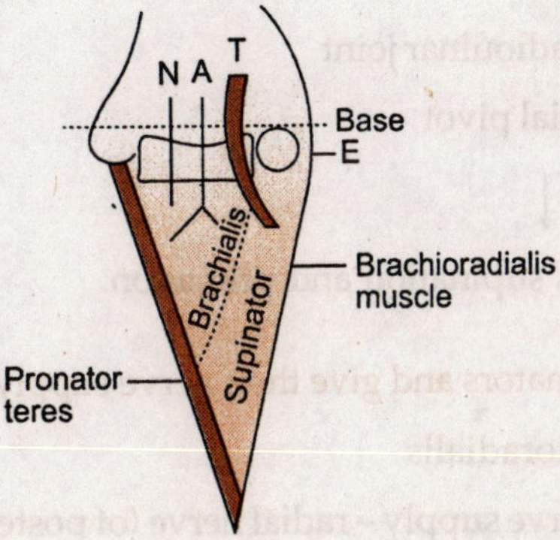

12. Name the muscles supplied by radial nerve.

Ans. 1. Three heads of Triceps brachii.

2. Anconeus
3. Brachioradialis
4. Brachialis partly
5. Extensor carpi radialis

13. Radioulnar joints:

Ans. Superior radioulnar joint – synovial

Variety – pivot

Movements – supination

\+

pronation

Middle radioulnar joint – two shafts are connected by interosseous membrane

Joint is fibrous

No movements

Inferior radioulnar joint

Synovial pivot

↓

allows supination and pronation.

14. Name supinators and give their nerve supply.

Ans. 1. Brachioradialis

Nerve supply – radial nerve (of posterior cord)

2. Biceps brachii

Nerve supply – musculocutaneous nerve (of lateral cord)

3. Supinator

Nerve supply – posterior interosseous nerve

↓

branch of radial nerve

15. Name pronators and give their nerve supply.

Ans. 1. Brachioradialis

Nerve supply – radial nerve

Pronator teres – median nerve

Pronator quadratus – anterior interosseous branch of median nerve

16. Enumerate the movements of pectoral girdle or shoulder girdle.

Ans. 1. Elevation of scapula

2. Depression of scapula
3. Protraction
4. Retraction
5. Rotation – Serratus anterior and Trapezius

17. Name the joints of shoulder girdle. What type of joints are they ?

Ans. 1. Sternoclavicular — saddle synovial joint

2. Acromioclavicular joint — plane synovial joint

Which part of body moves on above joints, i.e. scapula moves.

18. Enumerate the movements of shoulder joint.

Ans. 1. Flexion 2. Extension

3. Adduction 4. Abduction

5. Medial rotation 6. Lateral rotation

7. Circumduction

19. Name the muscles involved in abduction of shoulder joint. Give their nerve supply.

Ans. 0 to 20 degree by Supraspinatus.

20 to 90 degree by deltoid – middle of acromial fibres of Deltoid.

Above 90 degree – above head abduction

By Serratus anterior and Trapezius

Nerve supply: Supraspinatus by suprascapular nerve

Deltoid by axillary nerve

Serratus anterior by long thoracic nerve (nerve to serratus anterior)

Trapezius — by accessory nerve

20. Enumerate the movements of fingers and where they take place.

Ans. Fingers move on metacarpophalangeal joints.

Flexion – Lumbricals

– Flexor digitorum superficialis

– Flexor digitorum profundus

Extension – Extensor digitorum

– Interossei

– Lumbricals

Adduction – By Palmar interossei

Abduction – By Dorsal interossei

21. Give OINA of lumbricals in hand.

Ans. The lumbricals are small four slender muscles in the central part of palm of hand.

O – They originate from radial side of the tendons of flexor digitorum profundus.

I – Extensor expansion

N.S. – Lumbrical first and second by median nerve. Lumbrical third and fourth by deep branch of ulnar nerve.

Action– Flexion of metacarpophalangeal deep joints and extension of interphalangeal joints as they are inserted on dorsal digital expansion.

Flexor surface of fingers — showing origin of lumbricals:

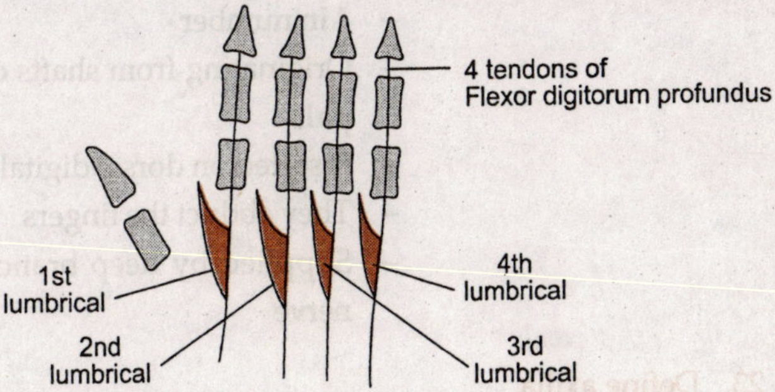

Dorsum of fingers – dorsal digital expansion:

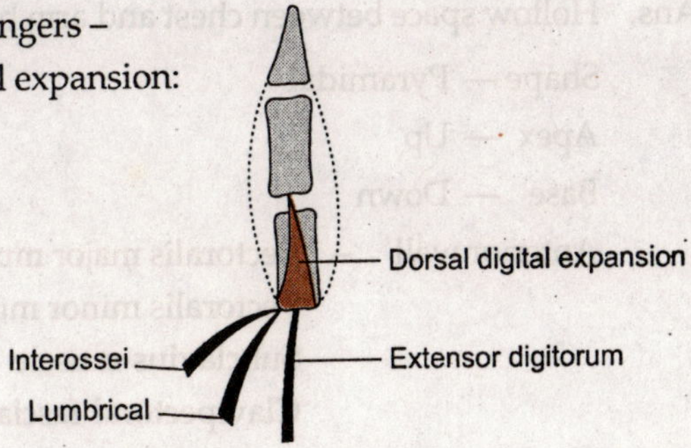

22. Describe interossei in hand.

Ans. Interossei are eight in number.

Four palmar and four dorsal.

They are in between metacarpal bones, so called interossei.

Palmar interossei
- Unipennate
- 4 in number
- Originating from shafts of the metacarpals
- Inserted on dorsal digital expansion
- They adduct the fingers
- Supplied by deep branch of ulnar nerve

Dorsal interossei
- Bipennate
- 4 in number
- Originating from shafts of metacarpals
- Inserted on dorsal digital expansion
- They abduct the fingers
- Supplied by deep branch of ulnar nerve

23. Define axilla.

Ans. Hollow space between chest and arm boundaries.

Shape — Pyramidal

Apex — Up

Base — Down

Anterior wall – Pectoralis major muscle
Pectoralis minor muscle
Subclavius muscle
Clavipectoral fascia

Posterior wall – Subscapularis muscle
Teres major muscle
Latissimus dorsi

Medially – Serratus anterior muscle

Laterally – Coracobrachialis muscle
Biceps brachii muscle

Apex is called cervicoaxillary canal

Anteriorly – Lies clavicle

Posteriorly – Scapula

Medially – First rib

Cervicoaxillary canal

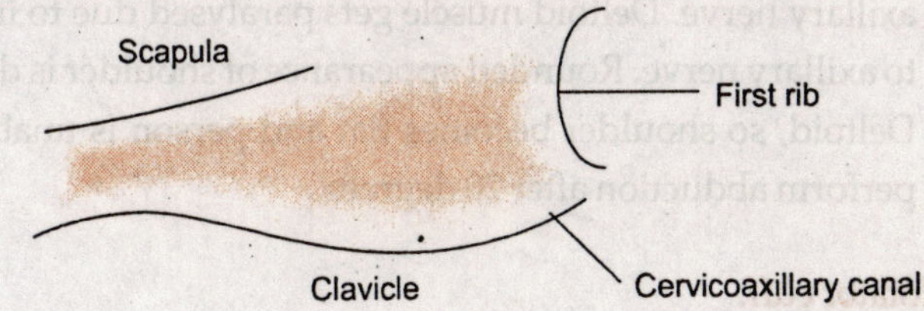

Base – Skin
– Superficial fascia
– Fat

Contents of axilla

1. Axillary artery and its branches
2. Axillary vein and its tributaries
3. Cords and branches of brachial plexus, i.e. intraclavicular part of brachial plexus
4. Axillary lymph nodes
5. Axillary pad of fat.

24. Factors of stability of shoulder joint.

Ans. 1. Coracoacromial arch

2. Tendon of long head of Biceps

3. Glenoidale labrum

4. Long head of Triceps tendon

5. Rotator cuff

All these factors keep the contact of head of humerus with glenoid cavity of scapula and also provide strength to capsule of shoulder. The capsule is having no direct support inferiorly and also capsule is loose inferiorly, hence inferior dislocation of shoulder is very common. This inferior dislocation is also called as subglenoid dislocation. This injures axillary nerve. Deltoid muscle gets paralysed due to injury to axillary nerve. Rounded appearance of shoulder is due to Deltoid, so shoulder becomes flat and person is unable to perform abduction after 20 degrees.

25. Rotator cuff.

Ans. This is one of the factor of stability to shoulder joint. This is made up of 4 insertions to capsule of shoulder joint. Capsule is made strong by these 4 muscle insertions fusing with capsule.

Anteriorly – Subscapularis muscle

Superiorly – Supraspinatus muscle

Posteriorly – Infraspinatus muscle

– Teres minor muscle

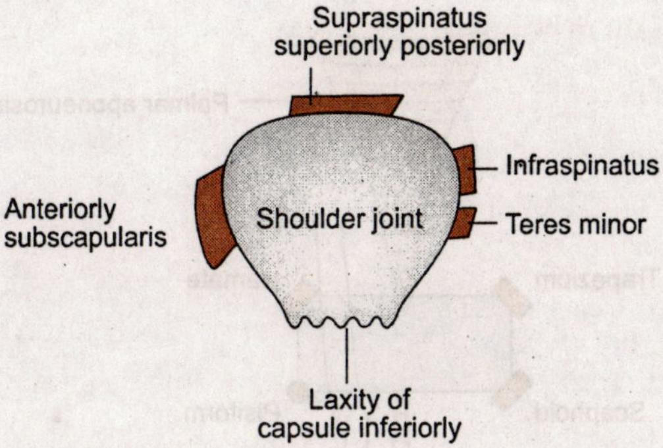

Importance of loose capsule inferiorly, i.e. person can do abduction freely.

26. Flexor retinaculum.

Ans. The thick band of deep fascia in front of wrist.

2 borders – Upper border – Palmaris longus is inserted

– Lower border – apex of palmar aponeurosis is attached

2 surfaces – 1. Superficial 2. Deep

Attached – Medially – a. Pisiform b. Hamate bone

Laterally – a. Scaphoid b. Trapezium

Ulnar nerve and ulnar artery lie superficial to flexor retinacular.

Median nerve, 4 tendons of Flexor digitorum superficialis and 4 tendons of flexor lie deep to flexor retinaculum.

Digitorum profundus

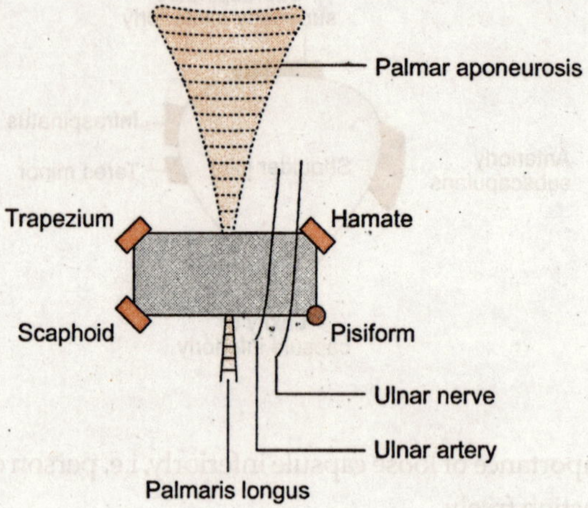

Deep to flexor retinaculum

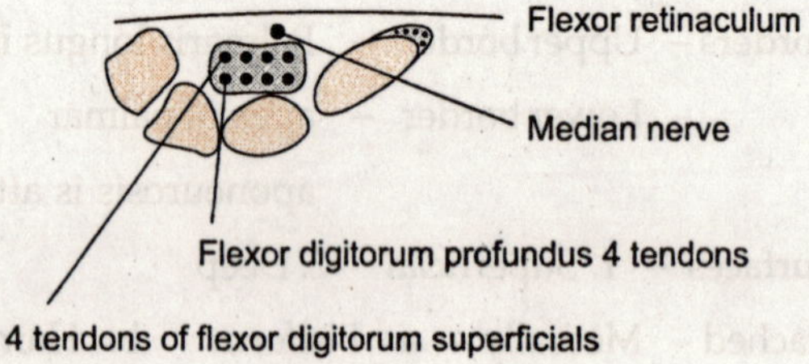

These tendons are enclosed in one synovial sheath.

27. Dorsal digital expansion:

Ans. A triangular fibrous structure on the dorsum of proximal phalanx. This provides insertion to 3 muscles:

1. Extensor digitorum
2. Lumbricals
3. Interossei

This triangular structure is connected with middle phalanx at its apex and with terminal phalanx with two collaterals.

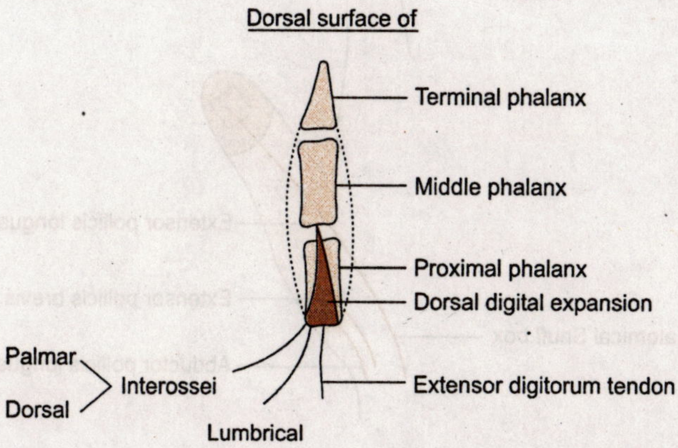

28. Anatomical snuff box:

Ans. Depression at the back of root of the thumb.

Studied in deeply extended thumb.

Posteriorly lies tendon of extensor Pollicis longus.

Anteriorly — Tendons of

1. Abductor pollicis longus
2. Extensor pollicis brevis

Contents:

1. Radial artery lies deep
2. Cephalic vein starts
3. Radial nerve gives cutaneous branches here

Deep in the space lies styloid process of radius.

Dorsal aspect of thumb shows anatomical snuff box.

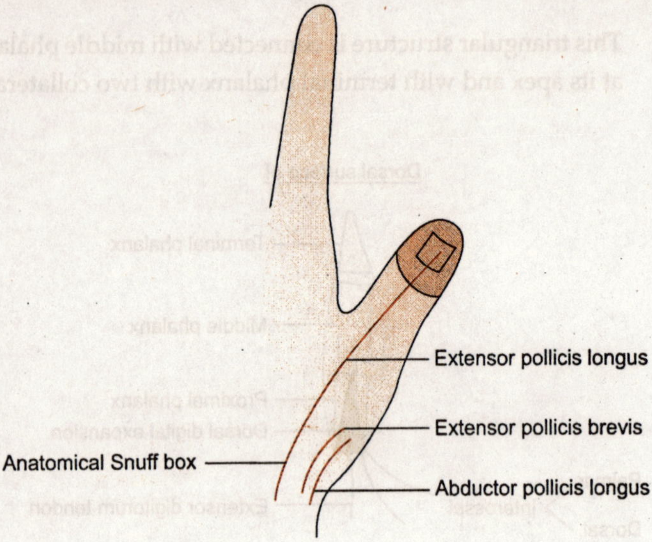

29. Carpal tunnel syndrome:

Ans. It is produced by compression of median nerve in carpal tunnel, i.e. space which lies deep to the flexor retinaculum.

It consists of 1. Burning pain in lateral 3½ fingers (palmar aspect)

2. Weakness of thenar muscles.

30. What are the movements of thumb ? Where thumb moves ? What are the types of joints ?

Ans. Thumb moves on carpometacarpal joint of thumb. The joint is saddle synovial joint.

The movements are:

1. Flexion
2. Extension
3. Abduction
4. Adduction

5. Medial rotation with flexion
6. Lateral rotation with extension
7. Opposition
8. Circumduction.

31. Enumerate the palmar spaces.

Ans. 1. Pulp space
2. Lumbrical spaces
3. Thenar space
4. Midpalmar space
5. Adductor space.

32. Give origin, insertion, nerve supply and action of biceps brachii.

Ans. This muscle lies in the anterior compartment of the arm.

O – It has – Long head arises from supraglenoid tubercle of scapula

It's origin is intracapsular and extrasynovial

– Short head – tip of the coracoid process of scapula (origin extracapsular)

I – Posterior part of radial tuberosity

N S – Musculocutaneous nerve

Branch of lateral cord of brachial plexus

Action – Flexion of shoulder joint

– Flexion of elbow joint

– Powerful supinator of forearm on superior radioulnar joint.

33. Name the joints of shoulder girdle. What type of joints are they ?

Ans. 1. Acromioclavicular joint — plane synovial joint.

2. Sternoclavicular joint — synovial saddle joint.

Chapter 5: Inferior Extremity

Multiple Choice Questions

1) Hip bone is:

a. Flat bone b. Irregular bone

c. Pneumatic bone d. None of the above

2) Lesser sciatic notch transmits following structures *except*:

a. Tendon of Obturator internus

b. Two gamelli muscles

c. Internal pudendal vessles

d. Tendon of Obturator externus

3) Structures at upper border of Piriformis muscle are:

a. Superior gluteal vessels

b. Superior gluteal nerve

c. Both of the above

d. None of the above

4) Femoral hernia passes through:

a. Femoral ring b. Superficial inguinal ring

c. Deep inguinal ring d. Inguinal canal

5) Lymph node on the femoral canal drains:

a. Scrotum b. Root of penis

c. Glans-penis d. Medial side of thigh

Ans. 1. b 2. d 3. c 4. a 5. c

6) **Obturator nerve innervates following muscles *except*:**

a. Adductor longus

b. Pectineus

c. Obturator externus

d. Obturator internus

7) **Deep fascia of thigh is:**

a. Dartos fascia b. Fascia lata

c. Fascia scarpa d. Fascia of Camper

8) **Articularis genu is supplied by:**

a. Obturator nerve b. Femoral nerve

c. Sciatic nerve d. None of the above

9) **Following is the component of hamstrings:**

a. Sartorius muscle

b. Semitendinosus and Semimembranosus muscle

c. Gracilis muscle

d. Pectineus muscle

10) **Iliotibial tract gives insertion to:**

a. Gluteus medius b. Gluteus maximus

c. Gluteus minimus d. None of the above

11) **Following muscle is not forming floor of femoral triangle:**

a. Pectineus b. Iliacus

c. Adductor longus d. Adductor magnus

Ans. 6. d 7. b 8. b 9. b 10. b 11. d

12) Following arteries arise from profunda femoris artery *except*:

a. Lateral circumflex femoral artery

b. Perforating branches

c. Descending genicular artery

d. Medial circumflex femoral artery

13) Femoral artery ends at:

a. Adductor tubercle

b. Apex of femoral triangle

c. Subsartorial or adductor canal

d. Opening of Adductor magnus

14) Following muscle has double nerve supply:

a. Sartorius b. Gracilis

c. Pectineus d. Iliacus

15) Following structure is not in adductor canal (subsartorial canal):

a. Femoral nerve b. Saphenous nerve

c. Femoral artery d. Femoral vein

16) What is true for Quadriceps femoris:

a. Powerful extensor of knee joint

b. Consists of 3 vasti and Rectus femoris

c. Patella develops in its tendon

d. All of the above

Ans. 12. c 13. d 14. c 15. a 16. d

17) Anterior superior iliac spine gives origin to:

a. Straight head of Rectus femoris
b. Reflected head of Rectus femoris
c. Sartorius
d. Gracilis

18) Contents of femoral sheath are:

a. Femoral artery, femoral vein and femoral nerve
b. Femoral artery and femoral nerve
c. Femoral vein and femoral nerve
d. Femoral artery and femoral vein

19) Gluteus maximus is showing all *except*:

a. Powerful extensor of hip joint
b. Supplied by femoral nerve
c. Inserted on gluteal tuberosity
d. Supplied by inferior gluteal nerve

20) Superior gluteal nerve supplies following muscles:

a. Gluteus medius b. Gluteus minimus
c. Tensor fascia lata d. All of the above

21) Following is not the part of hamstring:

a. Adductor magnus
b. Adductor longus
c. Semitendinosus
d. Semimembranosus

Ans. 17. c 18. a 19. b 20. d 21. b

22) Femoral nerve innervates following muscles:

a. Iliacus
b. Sartorius
c. Quadriceps femoris
d. All of the above

23) Tibial collateral ligament is the tendon of:

a. Adductor magnus
b. Adductor longus
c. Adductor brevis
d. Long head of Biceps

24) Following are the contents of popliteal fossa:

a. Popliteal artery
b. Popliteal vein
c. Sciatic nerve and its two terminal branches
d. All of the above

25) Peroneus longus has following facts:

a. Arises from upper 2/3 of lateral surface of fibula
b. Supplied by superficial peroneal nerve
c. Evert the foot
d. All of the above

26) Deep peroneal nerve supplies following muscles *except*:

a. Peroneus tertius
b. Peroneus brevis
c. Tibialis anterior
d. Extensor hallucis longus

27) Root value of femoral nerve is:

a. L 2, 3, 4
b. L 4, 5, S 1
c. S 1, 2, 3
d. S 2, 3, 4

Ans. 22. d 23. a 24. d 25. d 26. b 27. a

28) Tibialis posterior shows:

a. Inserted on the tuberosity of navicular bone

b. Does dorsiflexion of foot

c. Supplied by deep peroneal nerve

d. None of the above

29) Peripheral heart is:

a. Popliteus muscle

b. Sartorius muscle

c. Soleus muscle

d. Tendocalcaneus

30) Key muscle of knee is:

a. Sartorius   b. Popliteus

c. Soleus   d. None of the above

31). Tendocalcaneus is common tendon of:

a. Soleus

b. Both heads of Gastrocnemius

c. Both of the above

d. None of the above

32) Peroneal artery of peroneal compartment of leg is branch of:

a. Anterior tibial artery

b. Posterior tibial artery

c. Popliteal artery

d. Obturator artery

Ans. 28. a 29. c 30. b 31. c 32. b

33) Nerve to Popliteus arises from:

a. Sciatic nerve
b. Tibial nerve
c. Common peroneal nerve
d. None of the above

34) Dorsalis pedis shows:

a. Continuation of anterior tibial artery beyond ankle
b. Enters sole by passing between two heads of First dorsal interossei muscle
c. Both of the above
d. Continuation of posterior tibial artery

35) The ankle joint is:

a. Syndesmosis
b. Synovial hinge variety
c. Synovial plane variety
d. None of the above

36) Syndesmosis is:

a. Superior tibiofibular joint
b. Inferior tibiofibular joint
c. Subtalar joint
d. Ankle joint

37) Cruciate ligaments of knee are:

a. Extracapsular
b. Extrasynovial and intracapsular
c. Intrasynovial
d. None of the above

Ans. 33. b 34. c 35. b 36. b 37. b

38) Inversion and eversion are movements of foot on:

a. Ankle joint b. Subtalar joint

c. Midtarsal joint d. b + c

39) Lumbricals in the foot are:

a. Three b. Four

c. Five d. None of the above

40) Following muscles are in second layer of sole of foot:

a. Flexor digitorum longus tendon

b. Lumbricals

c. Flexor digitorum accessorius

d. All of the above

41) Number of plantar interossei in foot is:

a. Three b. Four

c. Five d. None of the above

42) Medial cuneiform bone receives insertion of:

a. Peroneus longus muscle

b. Tibialis anterior muscle

c. Both of the above

d. Tibialis posterior muscle

43) Great saphenous vein ascends:

a. In front of medial malleolus of tibia

b. Behind medial malleolus of tibia

c. In front of lateral malleolus of fibula

d. Behind lateral malleolus of fibula

Ans. 38. d 39. b 40. d 41. a 42. c 43. a

44) Ligament which supports the head of talus:

a. Deltoid ligament
b. Spring ligament
c. Long plantar ligament
d. Short plantar ligament

45) Following muscle invert the foot:

a. Tibialis anterior
b. Peroneus tertius
c. Tibialis posterior
d. a + c

46) Antegravity venous drainage from lower limbs mainly due to:

a. Muscular pump
b. Venous valves
c. Both of the above
d. None of the above

47) Pes cavus is a condition of foot in which:

a. Foot is flat
b. Foot is highly arched
c. Medially turned or inverted
d. Laterally turned or everted

48) Tibialis posterior is inserted on all tarsels *except*:

a. Calcaneus bone
b. Talus bone
c. Cuboid bone
d. Navicular bone

49) Main action of Peroneus longus is:

a. Plantar flexion
b. Dorsiflexion
c. Inversion
d. Eversion

Ans. 44. b 45. d 46. c 47. b 48. b 49. d

50) Oblique popliteal ligament is expansion derived from:

a. Semimembranous muscle

b. Semitendinous muscle

c. Popliteus muscle

d. Soleus muscle

51) Main role to maintain the arches of foot is by:

a. Spring ligament b. Plantar aponeurosis

c. Long tendons d. Short muscles of foot

52) Structures of knee joint helping as shock absorber are:

a. Cruciate ligaments

b. Semilunar cartilages

c. Ligamentum patellae

d. None of the above

53) Superior tibiofibular joint is:

a. Fibrous joint

b. Plane synovial joint

c. Saddle synovial joint

d. Condyloid synovial joint

54) Medial longitudinal arch is formed by following bones *except*:

a. Calcaneus b. Cuboid

c. Navicular d. Cuneiform

Ans. 50. a 51. b 52. b 53. b 54. b

55) Ligament of Bigelow belongs to:

a. Hip joint b. Knee joint

c. Ankle joint d. None of the above

56) Ligament which carries blood supply to head of femur is:

a. Transverse acetabular ligament

b. Ligamentum teres femoris

c. Iliofemoral ligament

d. None of the above

57) Ligament which limits extension is:

a. Iliofemoral ligament

b. Pubofemoral ligament

c. Ischiofemoral ligament

d. Ligamentum teres

58) Ligamentum patelle is continuation of:

a. Quadratus femoris b. Rectus femoris

c. Quadriceps femoris d. Biceps femoris

59) Linea aspera is the posterior border of:

a. Tibia b. Fibula

c. Femur d. None of the above

60) Nerve which is rolled at posterolateral aspect of neck of fibula is:

a. Tibial nerve b. Common peroneal nerve

c. Deep peroneal nerve d. Superficial peroneal nerve

Ans. 55. a 56. b 57. a 58. c 59. c 60. b

61) Sustentaculum tali is the part of:

a. Talus b. Navicular

c. Calcaneus d. Cuneiform

62) Poupart's ligament is:

a. Inguinal ligament

b. Sacrotuberous ligament

c. Spring ligament

d. Iliofemoral ligament

63) Following are functions of arches of foot *except*:

a. Support body weight

b. Walking on uneven surface

c. Provide elasticity to the foot

d. Increases efficiency of foot for walking, running

64) Important event at midinguinal point is:

a. Starting of femoral nerve

b. Site of femoral canal

c. Starting of femoral artery

d. End of great saphenous vein in femoral vein

65) Straight head of Rectus femoris is attached to:

a. Anterior superior iliac spine

b. Anterior inferior iliac spine

c. Pubic tubercle

d. Ischial spine

Ans: 61. c 62. a 63. a 64. c 65. b

66) Rider's bone is:

a. Patella

b. Ossified tendon of origin of Adductor longus

c. Pubis of hip bone

d. None of the above

67) Traction epiphysis is for:

a. Head of femur

b. Greater trochanter of femur

c. Lesser trochanter of femur

d. b + c

68) Subsartorial canal is:

a. Interosseus space

b. Intermuscular space for femoral vessels

c. Interfascial space

d. None of the above

69) Foot drop is due to injury to:

a. Sciatic nerve b. Tibial nerve

c. Common peroneal nerve d. a + b

70) Following muscle is accessory evertor of foot:

a. Peroneus tertius muscle

b. Peroneus brevis muscle

c. Peroneus longus muscle

d. Tibialis posterior muscle

Ans. 66. b 67. d 68. b 69. c 70. a

71) Following statement is true for Tibialis anterior muscle:

a. Does dorsiflexion of foot

b. Inverter of foot

c. Supplied by deep peroneal nerve

d. All of the above

72) Following statement is true for Peroneus longus *except*:

a. Evertor of foot

b. Supplied by superficial peroneal nerve

c. Maintain the lateral longitudinal arch of foot

d. Helps in dorsiflexion of ankle

73) Adductor magnus is supplied by:

a. Femoral nerve

b. Sciatic nerve

c. Obturator and sciatic nerve

d. Obturator nerve

74) Root value of sciatic nerve is:

a. L 4, 5, S 1, 2, 3 b. S 2, 3, 4

c. S 1, 2, 3 d. L 5, S 1, 2

75) What is third trochanter of femur:

a. Greater trochanter

b. Lesser trochanter

c. Gluteal tuberosity

d. Adductor tubercle

Ans. 71. d 72. d 73. c 74. a 75. c

76) Following is the sesamoid bone:

a. Fabella b. Fibula

c. Patella d. a + c

77) Following bone is stronger bone of leg:

a. Tibia

b. Fibula

c. Both of the above

d. None of the above

78) At midinguinal point, important feature is:

a. Palpate femoral nerve

b. Pulsations of femoral artery

c. Palpate the head of femur

d. Lies femoral canal

79) Saphenous nerve arises from:

a. Anterior division of obturator nerve

b. Anterior division of femoral nerve

c. Posterior division of femoral nerve

d. Posterior division of obturator nerve

80) Great saphenous vein joins with:

a. External iliac vein

b. Femoral vein

c. Popliteal vein

d. None of the above

Ans. 76. d 77. a 78. b 79. c 80. b

81) Inguinal ligament is attached to:

a. Anterior superior iliac spine and pubic tubercle

b. Anterior inferior iliac spine to pubic crest

c. Anterior superior iliac spine to pubic symphysis

d. None of the above

82) Medial longitudinal arch is formed by following bones *except*:

a. Cuboid
b. Calcaneus
c. Talus
d. Navicular

83) Lateral longitudinal arch is formed by following bones *except*:

a. Cuboid
b. Calcaneus
c. Navicular
d. 4th/5th metatarsals

84) Ventral 2/3 segment of iliac crest gives attachment to following muscles *except*:

a. External oblique

b. Internal oblique

c. Tensor fascia lata

d. Gluteus maximus

85) Following muscles are inserted on linea aspera *except*:

a. Adductor magnus
b. Sartorius
c. Adductor brevis
d. Adductor longus

Ans. 81. a 82. a 83. c 84. d 85. b

86) Quadratus femoris does:

a. Medial rotation of thigh
b. Lateral rotation of thigh
c. Flexion of thigh
d. Extension of thigh

Ans. 86. b

Short Answer Questions

1. Femoral sheath – Define. Name the compartments.

Ans. Funnel-shaped sheath of fascia for first 4 cm part of femoral artery and femoral vein is called femoral sheath.

Wide part of funnel is towards inguinal ligament. Narrow part of funnel fuses with the walls of femoral artery and femoral vein.

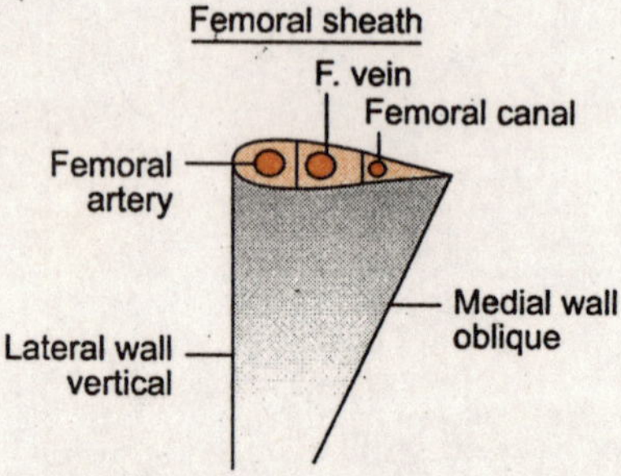

The sheath has 3 compartments:

– Lateral compartment contains femoral artery
– Middle compartment contains femoral vein
– Medial compartment is femoral canal.

Note: No sheath for femoral nerve.

2. Name the components of Quadriceps femoris. Give nerve supply. What is the action on knee ?

Ans. Components – Rectus femoris
– Vastus lateralis
– Vastus intermedius
– Vastus medialis

Nerve supply — By post.division of femoral nerve.

Action — Powerful extensor of knee.

3. Subsartorial canal (adductor canal – Hunter's canal).

Ans. This is in the middle of front of thigh.

This is intermuscular space for femoral artery and femoral vein.

Roofed by Sartorius muscle.

Floor – Adductor longus in the upper part

Adductor magnus in lower part

Medially – Vastus medialis

Contents – Femoral artery

– Femoral vein

– Saphenous nerve

– Nerve to Vastus medialis

TS of the middle of thigh

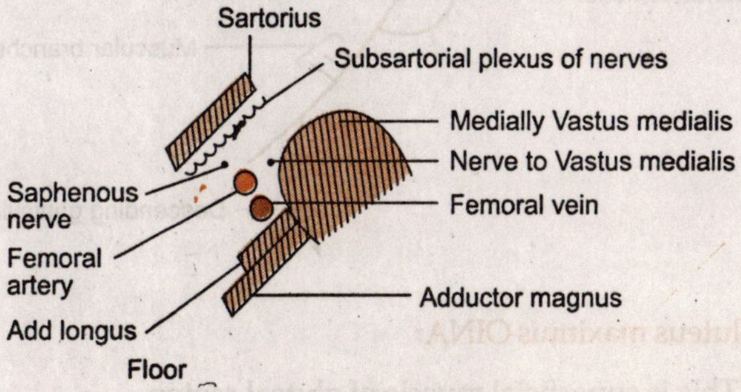

4. Name the branches of femoral artery.

Ans. 1. Three superficial

a. Superficial epigastric artery

b. Superficial circumflex iliac artery

c. Superficial external pudendal artery

2. Four muscular branches

3. Three deep

a. Deep external pudendal artery

b. Profunda femoris artery — in female

c. Descending genicular — in subsartorial canal

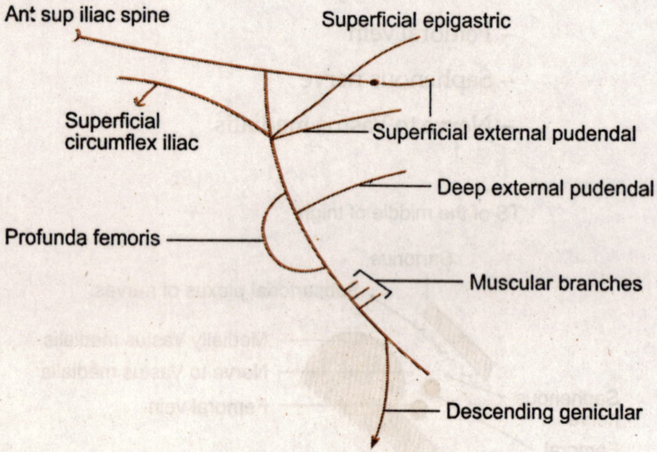

5. Gluteus maximus OINA:

Ans. This is superficial muscle of gluteal region.

It is powerful extensor of hip joint.

Origin – Sacrum

Coccyx

Sacrotuberous ligament

Dorsal 1/3 of iliac crest

Insertion – Superficial is inserted on iliotibial tract

– Deep on gluteal tuberosity of femur

N.S. – Inferior gluteal nerve – branch of sacral plexus

L 5, S 1, 2

6. Name the two abductors of hip joint and give their nerve supply.

Ans. Gluteus medius

Gluteus minimus

N.S. – Superior gluteal nerve (L 4, 5, S 1)

↓

Branch of sacral plexus

7. Name the structures passing through greater sciatic notch.

Ans. 1. Piriformis muscle

2. At upper border of Piriformis

subgluteal vessels and superior gluteal nerve

3. At lower border of Piriformis

– Inferior gluteal vessels

– Inferior gluteal nerve

– Sciatic nerve

– Posterior cutaneous nerve of thigh

– Nerve to Quadratus femoris

– Nerve to Obturator internus

– Pudendal nerve

– Internal pudendal vessels

8. Define hamstrings. Name hamstrings. Give their nerve supply and action on knee joint.

Ans. Muscles attached to ischial tuberosity of hip bone are hamstring muscles.

They are 1. Semimembranous

2. Semitendinous muscle

3. Long head Biceps

4. Small part of Adductor magnus

All are supplied by tibial part of sciatic nerve.

They are flexors of knee joint.

9. Name the muscles supplied by obturator nerve.

Ans. Anterior division – Pectineus

Adductor longus

Gracilis

Adductor brevis

Articular branch to hip joint

Posterior division – Obturator externus

Adductor magnus

Adductor brevis

Knee joint

10. Name structures passing through lesser sciatic notch.

Ans.
- Tendon of Obturator internus
- Pudendal nerve
- Internal pudendal vessels
- Origin of Gamelli – Superior gamellus
  – Inferior gamellus

11. Name the intra-articular structures of knee joint.

Ans. 1. Anterior cruciate ligament
2. Posterior cruciate ligament
3. Lateral meniscus
4. Medial meniscus
5. Tendon of Popliteus
6. Fat.

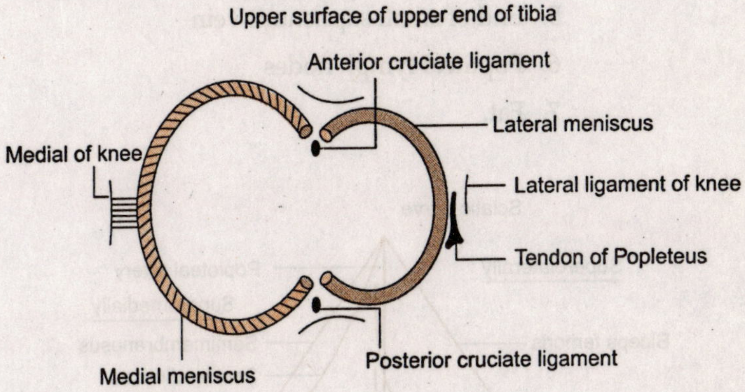

12. Popliteal fossa.

Ans. Definition – Hollow behind knee is popliteal fossa

Shape – Diamond-shaped

Boundaries – 2 superior – Superolaterally – tendon of Biceps femoris
– Superomedially – Semitendinous and Semimembranous

2 inferior – Inferomedially – medial head of Gastrocnemius
– Inferolaterally – lateral head of Gastrocnemius

Floor – Popliteal surface of femur capsule of knee joint
– Popliteus muscle and fascia covering Popliteus muscle

Contents: 1. Popliteal artery and its branches
2. Popliteal vein and its tributaries
3. Tibial nerve
4. Common peroneal nerve
5. End of small saphenous vein
6. Popliteal lymph nodes
7. Fat.

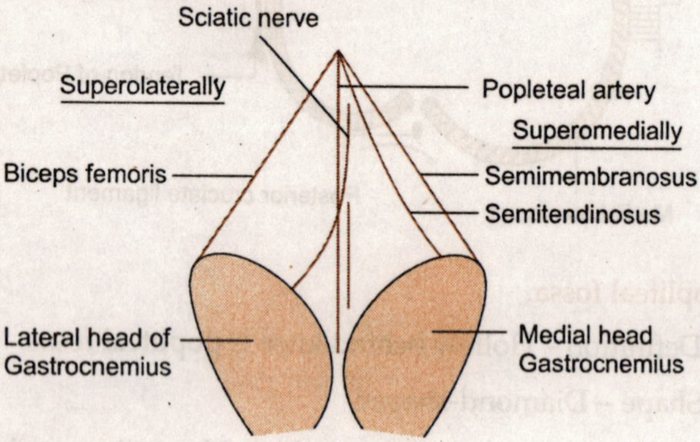

13. Enumerate the branches of popliteal artery.

Ans. 1. Superior medial genicular
2. Superior lateral genicular
3. Middle genicular
4. Inferior medial genicular
5. Inferior lateral genicular

6. Muscular branches
7. Terminal branches – two – anterior tibial artery
   – posterior tibial artery

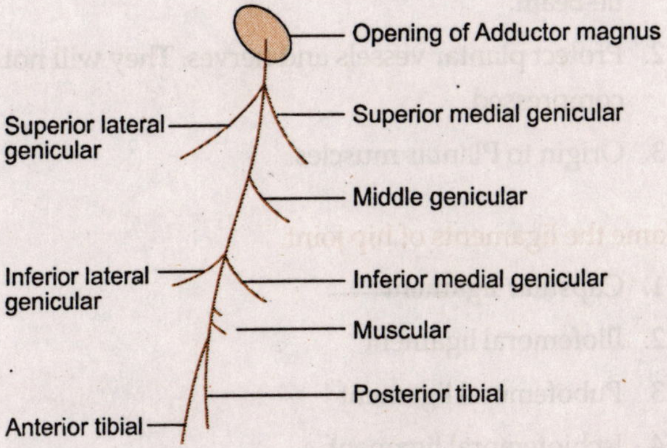

14. What type of joint is ankle joint ?

Ans. Synovial hinge

Bones taking part

– Lower end of tibia

+ medial malleolus of tibia

+ lateral malleolus of fibula

and

– Superior surface of body of talus — Trochlear surface

Most stable position of ankle — dorsiflexed

Least stable position — plantar flexed

15. What is plantar aponeurosis ? Give its functions.

Ans. Thick band of deep fascia deep to the skin of sole

– Triangular

– Posteriorly attached to tuberosity of calcaneus

Anteriorly to heads of metatarsals.

Function:

1. Maintains longitudinal arches of foot — acts as tie-beam.
2. Protect plantar vessels and nerves. They will not get compressed.
3. Origin to Plantar muscles.

16. Name the ligaments of hip joint.

Ans. 1. Capsular ligament

2. Iliofemoral ligament
3. Pubofemoral ligament
4. Ischiofemoral ligament
5. Ligamentum teres
6. Transverse acetabular ligament
7. Acetabular labrum.

17. Name two evertors and give their nerve supply.

Ans. 1. Peroneus longus muscle

2. Peroneus brevis muscle

N.S. – Superficial peroneal nerve (branch of sciatic nerve)

18. Name two invertors and give nerve supply.

Ans. 1. Tibialis anterior

N.S. – Deep peroneal nerve

2. Tibialis posterior

N.S. – Post-tibial nerve

19. What is fascia lata ?

Ans. Deep fascia of thigh is called fascia lata.

Two modifications – Iliotibial tract
– Cribriform fascia

20. Give OINA of muscles inserted on iliotibial tract.

Ans. Gluteus maximus – N.S. – inferior gluteal nerve
– Powerful extensor of hip
– Inserted on iliotibial tract and gluteal tuberosity of femur

Tensor fascia lata – Inserted on iliotibial tract
– Supplied by superior gluteal nerve
– Fascia lata is tensed during extension of knee
– It assists in extension of knee

21. Give the root value of sciatic nerve. Name any two muscles supplied by tibial part of sciatic nerve.

Ans. Root value L 4, 5 S 1, 3

Muscles supplied – Semimembranous
– Semitendinosus

22. Give functions of arches of foot.

Ans.
- They make the foot efficient for walking, running
- Acts as lever to propel the body forward during walking and running
- Concavity accommodates the blood vessels and nerve and protects them from pressure.

23. Name the joints related to hip bone.

Ans. Hip joint – Synovial – ball and socket

Pubic symphysis – Secondary cartilaginous joint

Sacroiliac – Plane synovial

In the walls of acetabulum 3 parts of bones, this bone unite in Y-shaped cartilage.

24. Define iliotibial tract. Name the muscles inserted on it. Give the nerve supply of those muscles.

Ans. The iliotibial tract is thick band of deep fascia on lateral side of thigh.

Attached to– Iliac crest – ventral 2/3rd segment (outer lip)

– Lateral condyle of tibia

Muscles inserted on it– Gluteus maximus superficial 3/4th part

N.S.: inferior gluteal nerve

– Tensor fascia lata

N.S.: superior gluteal nerve

25. Profunda femoris artery and its branches:

Ans. This is the branch of femoral artery which arises in femoral triangle.

The artery goes behind in back of thigh between Pectineus and Adductor longus.

Branches:

1. Lateral circumflex femoral artery
2. Medial circumflex femoral artery

Arise in femoral triangle.

3. Perforating branches:

   1st
   2nd | Perforate Adductor brevis
   3rd

   4th perforating is continuation of profunda

4. Muscular branches:

   To – hamstrings
   – adductors

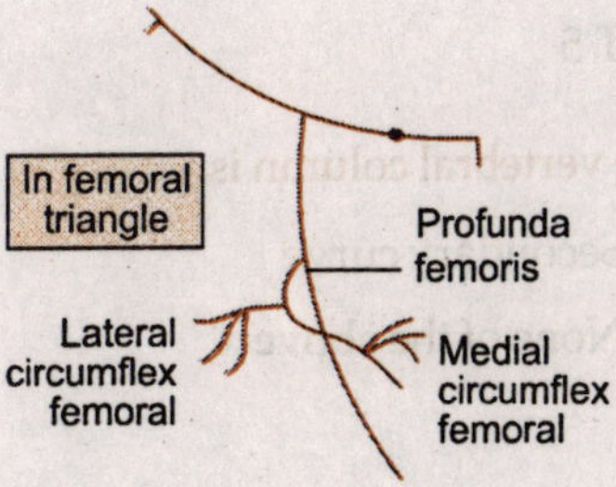

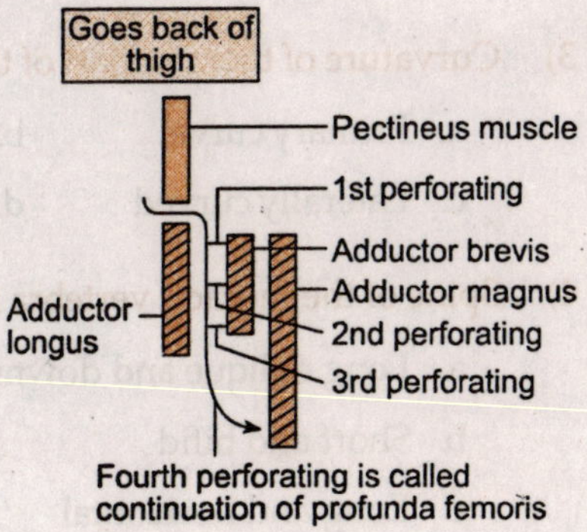

Chapter 6: Thorax

Multiple Choice Questions

1) The following bone is flat-bone:

   a. Scapula
   b. Sternum
   c. Ribs
   d. All of the above

2) Sternal angle corresponds with the lower border of:

   a. T 2
   b. T 4
   c. T 3
   d. T 5

3) Curvature of thoracic part of the vertebral column is:

   a. Primary curve
   b. Secondary curve
   c. Laterally curved
   d. None of the above

4) Spine of the thoracic vertebra is:

   a. Long oblique and downwards
   b. Short and bifid
   c. Long and horizontal
   d. Quadrangular

5) Following is the important landmark for counting the ribs:

   a. Jugular notch
   b. Sternal angle
   c. Xiphisternal joint
   d. Tip of the xiphoid process

Ans. 1. d 2. b 3. a 4. a 5. b

6) How many pairs of ribs are called as true ribs ?

a. Upper six
b. Upper seven
c. Upper five
d. Lower five

7) Following ribs are floating ribs:

a. 11th and 12th
b. 1st and 2nd
c. 10th and 11th
d. 9th and 10th

8) Which rib is the longest rib ?

a. 6th
b. 8th
c. 9th
d. 7th

9) Following changes take place at the level of sternal angle:

a. Trachea bifurcates
b. Beginning and end of arch of aorta
c. Second costal cartilage articulates
d. All of the above

10) Hilum of right lung shows:

a. Two pulmonary veins
b. Pulmonary artery
c. Eparterial and hyparterial bronchus
d. All of the above

11) How many bronchopulmonary segments are for right lung ?

a. Eight
b. Nine
c. Ten
d. None of the above

Ans. 6. b 7. a 8. d 9. d 10. d 11. c

12) Which part of aorta lies in superior mediastinum ?

a. Ascending aorta

b. Arch of aorta

c. Descending thoracic aorta

d. All of the above

13) Thymus lies in:

a. Superior mediastinum

b. Anterior mediastinum

c. Middle mediastinum

d. Posterior mediastinum

14) Splanchnic nerves are present in:

a. Anterior mediastinum

b. Middle mediastinum

c. Posterior mediastinum

d. Superior mediastinum

15) Posterior to trachea lies:

a. Thoracic duct b. Oesophagus

c. Arch of aorta d. None of the above

16) Fibrous and serous pericardium is supplied by:

a. Phrenic nerve

b. Vagus nerve

c. Sympathetic nerve

d. Splanchnic nerve

Ans. 12. b 13. a 14. c 15. b 16. a

17) Apex of heart is formed by:

a. Left atrium
b. Left ventricle
c. Right ventricle
d. None of the above

18) Adult apex beat is felt at:

a. Left fifth intercostal space
b. Left fourth intercostal space
c. Seventh intercostal space
d. Sixth intercostal space

19) Fossa ovalis is present in:

a. Right ventricle
b. Left ventricle
c. Right atrium
d. Left atrium

20) Right atrioventricular valve is:

a. Tricuspid valve
b. Mitral valve
c. Semilunar valve
d. Thebesian valve

21) Limbus fossa ovalis represents:

a. Septum primum
b. Septum secundum
c. Septum intermedius
d. None of the above

22) Following structure is called as pacemaker of heart:

a. S A node
b. A V node
c. Bundle of His
d. Purkinje fibres

Ans. 17. b 18. a 19. c 20. a 21. b 22. a

23) Root value of phrenic nerve is:

a. C 1, 2, 3
b. C 3, 4, 5
c. C 2, 3
d. C 3, 4

24) Base of heart is by:

a. 1/3 by right atrium
b. 2/3 by left atrium
c. a + b
d. Right ventricle

25) Oblique sinus of pericardium lies:

a. Posterior to right atrium
b. Anterior to left atrium
c. Posterior to right ventricle
d. Posterior to left atrium

26) Left border of heart is formed by:

a. Left atrium
b. Left auricle
c. Left ventricle and left auricle
d. Left ventricle

27) Which part of oesophagus shows striated and nonstriated muscle ?

a. Upper one-third
b. Middle one-third
c. Lower one-third
d. None

28) Aortic opening in diaphragm transmits:

a. Aorta
b. Thoracic duct
c. Azygos vein
d. All of the above

Ans. 23. b 24. c 25. d 26. c 27. b 28. d

29) Following are the opening in right atrium *except*:

a. Superior vena cava
b. Inferior vena cava
c. Pulmonary veins
d. Coronary sinus

30) Two bronchial arteries are for:

a. Right lung b. Left lung
c. Both of the above d. None of the above

31) Oesophagus has:

a. Three constrictions
b. Four constrictions
c. Five constrictions
d. No constrictions

32) Following structure shows star-shaped lumen:

a. Trachea b. Oesophagus
c. Aorta d. Stomach

33) Hyaline cartilage is absent in:

a. Trachea b. Bronchus
c. Segmental bronchi d. Bronchioles

34) Following structure is lined by pseudostratified columnar ciliated epithelium:

a. Trachea b. Bronchi
c. Oesophagus d. a + b

Ans. 29. c 30. b 31. b 32. b 33. d 34. d

35) Elastic arteries are:

a. Aorta
b. Subclavian
c. Carotids
d. All of the above

36) The muscle arising from floor of costal groove is:

a. External intercostal muscle
b. Internal intercostal muscle
c. Intercostal intimus
d. None of the above

37) Costal groove is absent in:

a. Typical rib
b. Second rib
c. Twelfth rib
d. None of the above

38) Only veins in the body containing the oxygenated blood are:

a. Pulmonary veins
b. Superior vena cava
c. Coronary sinus
d. Inferior vena cava

39) Large sternocostal surface is for:

a. Right atrium
b. Right ventricle
c. Left ventricle
d. None of the above

40) Following are the branches of descending thoracic aorta *except*:

a. Posterior intercostal arteries
b. Superior phrenic arteries
c. Anterior intercostal arteries
d. Mediastinal branches

Ans. 35. d 36. b 37. c 38. a 39. b 40. c

Short Answer Questions

1. Fallot's tetralogy:

Ans. Includes:

1. Ventricular septal defect
2. Over-riding of aorta
3. Right-ventricular hypertrophy
4. Pulmonary stenosis.

2. Constrictions of oesophagus - (4):

Ans. 1st – pharyngo-oesophageal junction

2nd – where it is crossed by arch of aorta

3rd – where it is crossed by left bronchus

4th – where it pierces diaphragm.

They are measured from incisor teeth

6 inches from incisor teeth – first

9 inches from incisor teeth – second

11 inches from incisor teeth – third

15 inches from incisor teeth – fourth.

3. Name the four contents of posterior mediastinum.

Ans. 1. Oesophagus

2. Descending thoracic aorta and its branches
3. Azygos vein
4. Thoracic duct.

4. Name the tributaries of right atrium.

Ans. 1. Superior vena cava

2. Inferior vena cava

3. Coronary sinus

4. Anterior cardiac vein

5. Vena cordis minimi.

5. Define bronchopulmonary segments and their importance.

Ans. They are the well-defined sectors of lung tissue having tertiary bronchus. Each is triangular in shape.

Base towards periphery and apex towards hilum of lung.

Each has its – own bronchus

– own artery

– vein is intersegmental two for adjacent segments

Study of bronchopulmonary segments is important as during the removal of affected part is without disturbing normal lung tissue. Common infections are tuberculosis, malignancy.

6. Name pericardial sinuses.

Ans. • Transverse sinus of pericardium lies anterior to left atrium

• Oblique sinus lies post to left atrium.

7. Name the branches of arch of aorta.

Ans. 1. Brachiocephalic trunk

2. Left common carotid artery

3. Left subclavian artery.

8. Typical intercostal space:

Ans. Space in between two ribs of same side is intercostal space.

Space is closed by three strata of muscles:

1. External intercostal muscle
2. Internal intercostal muscle
3. Intercostal intimus muscle.

Contents:

1. Intercostal vein
2. Intercostal artery — Van
3. Intercostal nerve

Diagram of typical intercostal space:

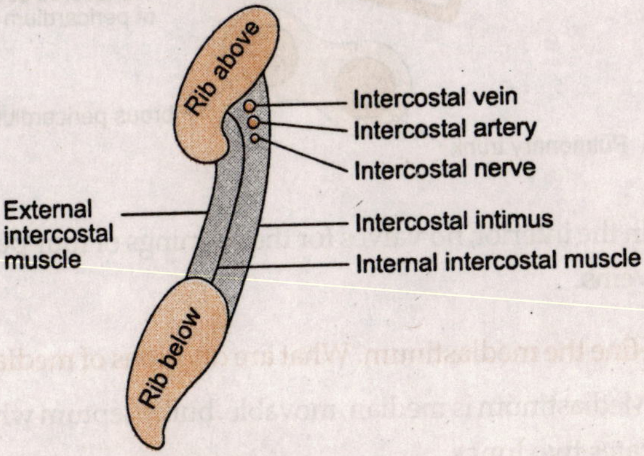

9. Left atrium and its tributaries:

Ans. Left atrium forms 2/3 base of heart.

– It is hidden due to

1. Aorta
2. Pulmonary trunk

– It is the most posterior part of heart

Posterior to it lies oblique sinus of pericardium.

Anterior to it lies transverse sinus of pericardium tributaries.

– four pulmonary veins – two from each lung

– vena cordis minimi

↓

small veins from walls of heart

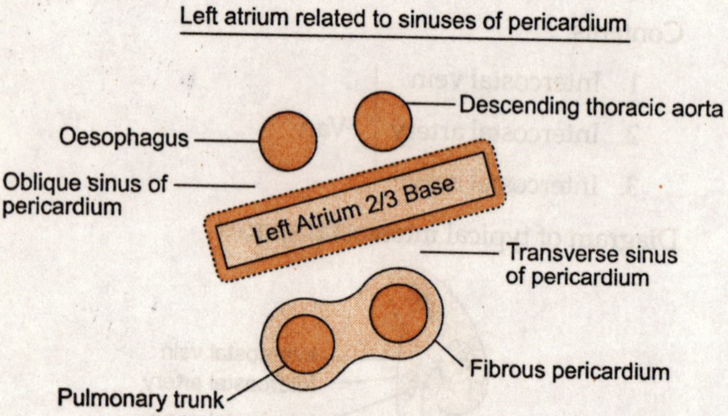

In the interior, no valves for the openings of four pulmonary veins.

10. Define the mediastinum. What are divisions of mediastinum ?

Ans. Mediastinum is median, movable, bulky septum which separates two lungs.

– The imaginary plane passes through sternal angle and lower border of 4th thoracic vertebra divides the mediastinum into:

– superior mediastinum — above the imaginary plane

– inferior mediastinum — below the imaginary plane

This again divides into:

- anterior mediastinum — anterior to heart
- middle mediastinum — occupied by heart
- posterior mediastinum — posterior to heart

11. Define root of lung. Name the structures in root of lung.

Ans. Root is the part of lung which is attached to mediastinum.

Structures:

1. Two pulmonary veins
2. Pulmonary artery
3. Bronchus
4. Bronchial arteries
5. Lymph nodes — bronchopulmonary lymph nodes
6. Sympathetic plexus around pulmonary artery is pulmonary plexus
7. Loose areolar tissue.

Root of right lung

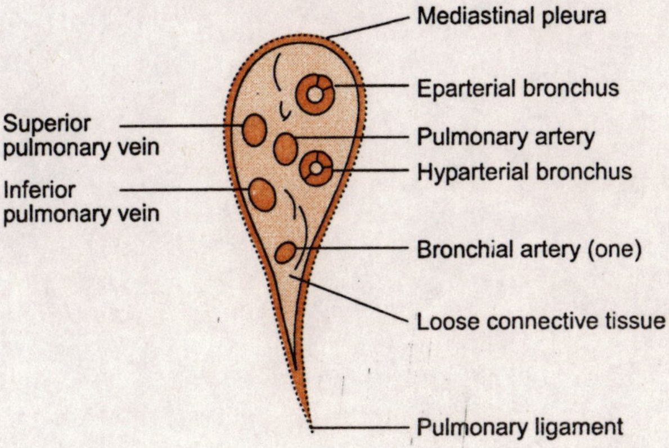

Root of left lung

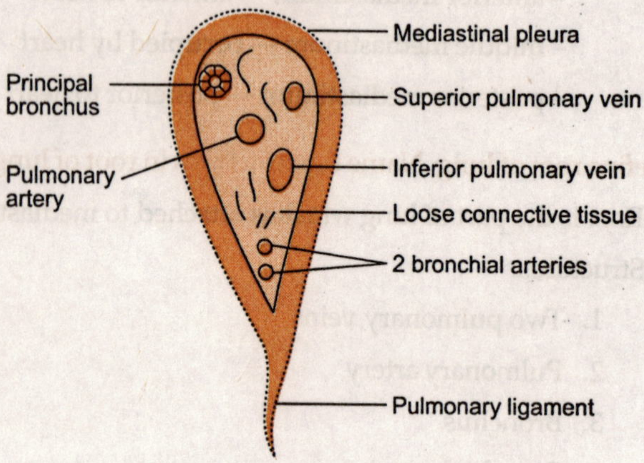

Chapter 7: Abdomen and Pelvis

Multiple Choice Questions

1) Umbilicus in adult lies at the level of intervertebral disc between:
   a. L 3 and L 4 vertebra
   b. L 2 and L 3 vertebra
   c. L 4 and L 5 vertebra
   d. L 1 and L 2 vertebra

2) Following are the muscles of anterior abdominal wall *except*:
   a. External oblique
   b. Internal oblique
   c. Serratus anterior
   d. Pyramidalis

3) Skin around umbilicus is supplied by:
   a. T 9 segment
   b. T 10 segment
   c. T 11 segment
   d. T 12 segment

4) Transpyloric plane lies at:
   a. Lower border of L 1 vertebra
   b. Upper border of L 2 vertebra
   c. Upper border of L 1 vertebra
   d. Upper border of L 3 vertebra

Ans. 1. a 2. c 3. b 4. a

5) Inguinal ligament is lower border of aponeurosis of:

a. Internal oblique muscle

b. External oblique muscle

c. Transversus abdominis

d. Rectus abdominis

6) Medial end of the inguinal ligament is attached to:

a. Anterior superior iliac spine

b. Pubic symphysis

c. Pubic crest

d. Pubic tubercle

7) Superficial inguinal ring is:

a. Triangular gap in external oblique aponeurosis

b. Oval opening in fascia transversalis

c. In the rectus sheath

d. None of the above

8) Following region shows no deep fascia:

a. Thigh

b. Sole of foot

c. Anterior abdominal wall

d. None of the above

9) Caput medusae is dilatation of veins around:

a. Lower end of oesophagus

b. Lower end of rectum

c. Around umbilicus

d. Base area of liver

Ans. 5. b 6. d 7. a 8. c 9. c

10) Following structures pass through inguinal canal *except*:

a. Spermatic cord in males
b. Round ligament of uterus in females
c. Ilioinguinal nerve
d. Pudendal nerve

11) Oval opening in fascia transversalis is:

a. Femoral ring
b. Superficial inguinal ring
c. Deep inguinal ring
d. None of the above

12) Triple role in inguinal canal boundaries is played by:

a. External oblique
b. Internal oblique
c. Transversus abdominis
d. Rectus abdominis

13) Inferior epigastric artery is branch of:

a. External iliac artery
b. Internal iliac artery
c. Femoral artery
d. None of the above

14) Following structures are at transpyloric plane *except*:

a. Origin of superior mesenteric artery
b. Origin of inferior mesenteric artery
c. Fundus of gallbladder
d. Pylorus of stomach

15) Lumbar curvature of the vertebral column is:

a. Primary curvature
b. Secondary curvature
c. Develops after birth
d. b + c

Ans. 10. d 11. c 12. b 13. a 14. b 15. d

16) At the level of 2nd lumbar vertebra lies:

a. Duodenojejunal junction

b. Cardiac end of stomach

c. Ileocaecal junction

d. None of the above

17) Rectus sheath contains following structures *except*:

a. Rectus abdominis

b. Rectus femoris

c. Lower five intercostal nerves

d. Anastomosis between superior and inferior epigastric arteries

18) At 4th lumbar vertebra following takes place:

a. Formation of portal vein

b. Bifurcation of aorta

c. Origin of interior mesenteric artery

d. Pyloric end of stomach

19) Inferior pancreaticoduodenal artery arises from:

a. Coeliac trunk

b. Superior mesenteric artery

c. Inferior mesenteric artery

d. None of the above

Ans. 16. a 17. b 18. b 19. b

20) Foregut artery is:

a. Coeliac trunk

b. Superior mesenteric artery

c. Inferior mesenteric artery

d. None of the above

21) Mobile end of stomach is:

a. Cardiac end
b. Pyloric end
c. Both of the above
d. None of the above

22) Greater curvature of stomach gives attachment to:

a. Greater omentum

b. Gastrosplenic ligament

c. Gastrophrenic ligament

d. All of the above

23) Gas containing part of stomach is:

a. Body
b. Pylorus
c. Fundus
d. Cardiac end

24) Stomach bed consists of following structures *except*:

a. Spleen
b. Splenic artery
c. Pancreas
d. Right kidney

25) Contents of lesser omentum of stomach is:

a. Portal vein
b. Bile duct
c. Hepatic artery
d. All of the above

Ans. 20. a 21. b 22. d 23. c 24. d 25. d

26) Following structure is called abdominal policeman:

a. Mesentery
b. Greater omentum
c. Lesser omentum
d. Transverse mesocolon

27) Duodenal cap is radiological shadow of:

a. First two inches part of duodenum
b. First one inch part of duodenum
c. Second part of duodenum
d. Third part of duodenum

28) Length of duodenum is:

a. 8 inches
b. 10 inches
c. 12 inches
d. 15 inches

29) Microscopically in duodenum seen are:

a. Peyer's patches
b. Solitary lymphatic follicles
c. Villi
d. Brunner's glands in submucosa

30) Common bile duct and pancreatic duct open in:

a. Posterolateral aspect of second part
b. Posteromedial aspect of second part
c. Third part of duodenum
d. First part of duodenum

Ans. 26. b 27. b 28. b 29. d 30. b

31) At third lumbar vertebra lies:

a. Third part of duodenum

b. Origin of inferior mesenteric artery

c. Both of the above

d. None of the above

32) Commonest position of vermiform appendix is:

a. Retrocaecal and retrocolic (12 o'clock)

b. Pelvic

c. Splenic

d. Paracolic

33) Porta hepatis of liver shows:

a. Portal vein b. Hepatic artery

c. Hepatic duct d. All of the above

34) Portal triad consists of following structures *except*:

a. Portal vein b. Hepatic artery

c. Bile duct d. Hepatic vein

35) Ligamentum teres hepatis is:

a. Obliterated right umbilical vein

b. Obliterated left umbilical vein

c. Obliterated right umbilical artery

d. Obliterated left umbilical artery

Ans. 31. c 32. a 33. d 34. d 35. b

36) Radiological photograph of gallbladder is:

a. Cholecystography b. Pyelography

c. Barium meal X-ray d. None of the above

37) The pancreas is:

a. Exocrine gland b. Endocrine gland

c. Both of the above d. None of the above

38) Following statements are true for uncinate process of head of pancreas:

a. Develops from ventral pancreatic bud

b. Arises from lower part of head

c. Related anterior to superior mesenteric blood vessels

d. All of the above

39) Long axis of hilum of spleen coincides with:

a. 9th rib b. 10th rib

c. 11th rib d. 12th rib

40) Formation of portal vein is behind:

a. Head of pancreas b. Neck of pancreas

c. Body of pancreas d. At porta hepatis of liver

41) The organ moving with respiration:

a. Kidney b. Liver

c. Spleen d. All of the above

Ans. 36. a 37. c 38. d 39. b 40. b 41. d

42) Hilum of spleen contains:

a. Splenic artery b. Splenic vein
c. Tail of pancreas d. All of the above

43) Following muscles are forming kidney bed *except*:

a. Psoas major
b. Quadratus lumborum
c. Transverse abdominis
d. Rectus abdominis

44) Mineralocorticoids are secreted by:

a. Zona fasciculata b. Zona glomerulosa
c. Zona reticularis d. None of the above

45) Following structure lies in the hilum of suprarenal gland:

a. Suprarenal vein
b. Superior suprarenal artery
c. Middle suprarenal artery
d. Inferior suprarenal artery

46) Descending colon develops from:

a. Foregut b. Midgut
c. Hindgut d. None of the above

47) Inferior vena caval opening in the diaphragm is at:

a. T 10 level b. T 12 level
c. T 8 level d. L 1 level

Ans. 42. d 43. d 44. b 45. a 46. c 47. c

48) Inferior mesenteric artery shows following features *except*:

a. It is midgut artery

b. Unpaired branch of abdominal aorta

c. Arises at L 3 level

d. Continues as superior rectal artery in the pelvis

49) Ureter shows:

a. Four constrictions b. Two constrictions

c. Five constrictions d. Three constrictions

50) Ureters are lined by:

a. Transitional epithelium

b. Stratified squamous nonkeratinised

c. Stratified columnar

d. None of the above

51) Only surface of urinary bladder covered by peritoneum is:

a. Superior surface b. Base

c. Inferolateral surfaces d. None of the above

52) Seminal vesicles are related to:

a. Base of urinary bladder

b. Superior surface

c. Neck

d. Inferolateral surface

Ans. 48. a 49. d 50. a 51. a 52. a

53) Trigone of urinary bladder is:

a. Ectodermal b. Mesodermal
c. Endodermal d. None of the above

54) Fixed part of urinary bladder is:

a. Apex b. Neck
c. Base d. All of the above

55) Following ligament is attached to apex of urinary bladder:

a. Median umbilical ligament
b. Lateral ligament
c. Pubovesical ligament
d. None of the above

56) Detrusor muscle is of:

a. Ureter b. Urethra
c. Urinary bladder d. Uterus

57) Most dilatable part of urethra is:

a. Penile of spongy urethra
b. Membranous part
c. External urethral orifice
d. Prostatic urethra

58) Narrowest part of urethra is:

a. External urethral orifice b. Internal urethral orifice
c. Membranous part d. None of the above

Ans. 53. b 54. b 55. a 56. c 57. d 58. a

59) Epididymis shows following features *except*:

a. Comma-shaped organ posterolateral to testes

b. Stores spermatozoa

c. Develops from mesonephric duct

d. Helps in spermatogenesis

60) Following are the contents of spermatic cord *except*:

a. Testicular artery b. Vas deferens

c. Testicular vein d. Pampiniform plexus of veins

61) Following are the coverings of testes *except*:

a. Tunica albuginea b. Tunica vasculosa

c. Tunica vaginalis d. Germinal epithelium

62) Testes develop from:

a. Genital tubercle b. Mesonephric duct

c. Genital ridge d. None of the above

63) Following cells of testes secrete testosterone:

a. Cells of Sertoli

b. Interstitial cells of Leydig

c. Spermatogenic cells

d. All of the above

64) Left testicular vein opens in:

a. Femoral vein b. Inferior vena cava

c. Left renal vein d. External iliac vein

Ans. 59. d 60. c 61. d 62. c 63. b 64. c

65) Following arteries are in spermatic cord *except*:

a. Scrotal vessels
b. Testicular artery
c. Artery of vas deferens
d. Cremasteric artery

66) Fascia transversalis of anterior abdominal wall continues on spermatic cord as:

a. External spermatic fascia
b. Internal spermatic fascia
c. Cremasteric fascia
d. None of the above

67) Genitofemoral branch of lumbar plexus supplies:

a. External oblique of abdomen
b. Cremaster muscle in males
c. Conjoint tendon
d. Pyramidalis

68) Which type of testes produce spermatozoa ?

a. Undescended
b. Descended in scrotum
c. Both of the above
d. None of the above

69) Fertilisation of ovum usually takes place in which part of uterine tube ?

a. Intramural part
b. Isthmus
c. Ampulla
d. Infundibulum

Ans. 65. a 66. b 67. b 68. b 69. c

70) Normal position of uterus is:

a. Anteverted and anteflexed

b. Retroverted

c. Retroflexed

d. Anteverted and retroflexed

71) Which surface of uterus is completely covered by peritoneum ?

a. Anterior surface
b. Posterior surface
c. Both of the above
d. None of the above

72) Paramesonephric duct forms:

a. Uterus
b. Uterine tubes
c. Cervix
d. All of the above

73) Uterine artery is paired and arise from:

a. External iliac artery
b. Internal iliac artery
c. Aorta
d. None of the above

74) Following structure is not the content of broad ligament:

a. Uterine tubes
b. Uterus
c. Ovaries
d. Ovarian artery

75) Ovarian artery arises from:

a. Abdominal aorta
b. Internal iliac artery
c. Uterine artery
d. None of the above

Ans. 70. a 71. b 72. d 73. b 74. c 75. a

76) Cervix of uterus is fixed by:

a. Pelvic diaphragm
b. Mackenrodt's ligament
c. Broad ligaments
d. None of the above

77) Joint between fifth lumbar vertebra and sacrum is:

a. Primary cartilaginous joint
b. Secondary cartilaginous joint
c. Syndesmosis
d. Plane synovial joint

78) Sacroiliac joint is:

a. Plane synovial joint
b. Secondary cartilaginous joint
c. Hinge synovial joint
d. Fibrous joint

79) Pubic symphysis is:

a. Primary cartilaginous joint
b. Secondary cartilaginous joint
c. Plane synovial joint
d. None of the above

80) Strongest ligament of the body is:

a. Ventral sacroiliac ligament
b. Dorsal sacroiliac ligament
c. Interosseous sacroiliac ligament
d. Sacrotuberous ligament

Ans. 76. b 77. b 78. a 79. b 80. c

81) Pectinate line indicates the:

a. Line at which anal valves are situated

b. Columnar epithelium changes to stratified squamous

c. Portal and systemic anastomosis

d. None of the above

82) Following muscle part has bony attachment:

a. Subcutaneous part of external sphincter of anal canal

b. Superficial part of exterior sphincter

c. Deep part of external sphincter

d. Internal sphincter

83) Following parts develop from hindgut:

a. Rectum

b. Upper 2/3 of anal canal

c. Pelvic colon

d. All of the above

84) External sphincter of anal canal is supplied by:

a. Pelvic splanchnic nerve

b. Hypogastric plexus

c. Pudendal nerve

d. None of the above

85) Pelvic diaphragm is formed by:

a. Levator ani

b. Coccygeus

c. Both of the above

d. None of the above

Ans. 81. a 82. b 83. d 84. c 85. c

86) Following nerves arise from lumbar plexus *except*:

a. Genitofemoral nerve b. Iliohypogastric nerve

c. Ilioinguinal nerve d. Pudendal nerve

87) Following is the midgut derivative:

a. Stomach b. Oesophagus

c. Appendix d. Upper 1/2 of duodenum

88) Following is the branch of posterior division of internal iliac artery:

a. Superior gluteal artery

b. Obturator artery

c. Middle rectal artery

d. Uterine artery in female

89) Uterine tubes are lined by:

a. Simple columnar ciliated

b. Simple columnar with microvilli

c. Simple columnar

d. Double columnar

90) Pudendal canal is in the:

a. Lateral wall of ischiorectal fossa

b. Medial wall of ischiorectal fossa

c. Near the apex of ischiorectal fossa

d. At base

Ans. 86. d 87. c 88. a 89. a 90. a

91) Rectum is showing following features:

a. From 3rd sacral vertebra to tip of coccyx
b. Continuation of pelvic colon
c. No sacculations
d. All of the above

92) Pancreatica magna artery arises from:

a. Superior mesenteric artery
b. Inferior mesenteric artery
c. Splenic artery
d. None of the above

93) Progesterone is secreted by:

a. Corpus luteum b. Corpus albicans
c. Ovarian follicles d. None of the above

94) Theca interna cells of ovary secretes:

a. Progesterone b. Oestrogen
c. Both of the above d. None of the above

95) Following structure is not developing from mesonephric duct:

a. Nephrons of kidney — secreting part
b. Collecting tubules
c. Vas deferens
d. Epididymis

Ans. 91. d 92. c 93. a 94. b 95. a

96) Following structure forms adult human kidney:

a. Pronephros b. Mesonephros
c. Metanephros d. Urogenital sinus

97) Vascular segments of kidney are:

a. Four b. Five
c. Six d. Three

98) Vas deferens has following features:

a. Content of spermatic cord
b. Develops from mesonephric duct
c. Star-shaped lumen
d. All of the above

99) MacBurney's point is related to:

a. Caecum b. Appendix
c. Colon d. Kidneys

100) Insulin secreting cells of pancreas are:

a. Pancreatic acini b. Alpha cells
c. Beta cells d. Delta cells

Ans. 96. c 97. b 98. d 99. b 100. c

Short Answer Questions

1. Epiploic foramen – Foramen of Winslow or aditus to lesser sac:

Ans. It is communication of greater and lesser sac of peritoneum.

This lies at T12 level.

Superiorly lies caudate lobe of liver

Inferiorly — first part of duodenum

Posteriorly — inferior vena cava

Anteriorly — portal vein

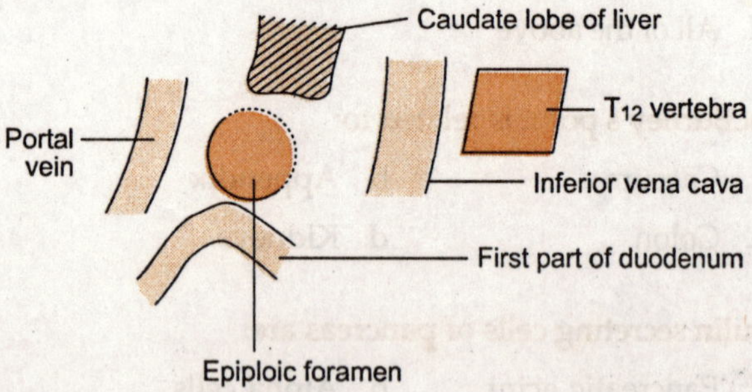

2. Name the parts of extrahepatic biliary apparatus.

Ans.
1. Right hepatic duct and left hepatic duct
2. Common hepatic duct
3. Gallbladder
4. Duct of gallbladder called cystic duct
5. Common hepatic duct and cystic duct unite to form common bile duct which opens in second part of duodenum.

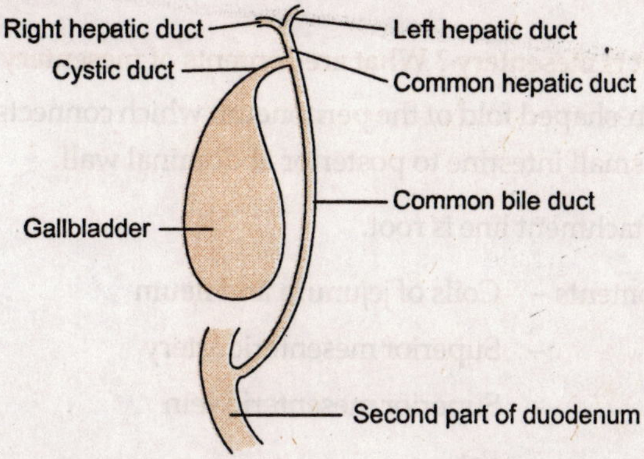

3. Enumerate the contents of spermatic cord.

Ans. 1. Main bulk is by pampiniform plexus of veins
2. Vas deferens
3. Artery of vas deferens
4. Testicular artery
5. Cremasteric artery
6. Lymphatics from testes
7. Genital branch of genitofemoral nerve
8. Sympathetic nerve plexus.

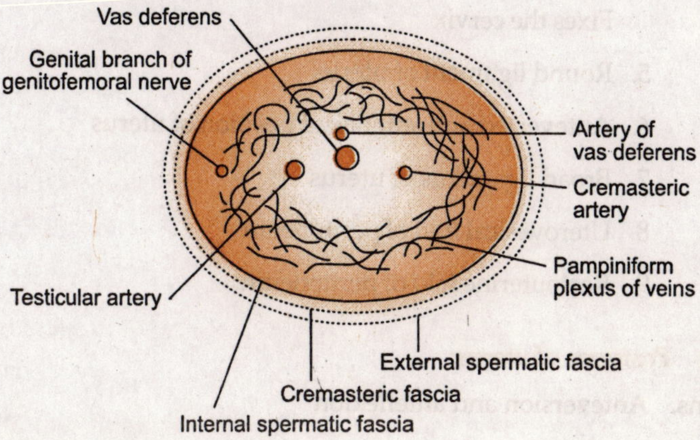

4. **What is mesentery ? What are contents of mesentery ?**

Ans. Fan-shaped fold of the peritoneum which connects the coils of small intestine to posterior abdominal wall.

Attachment line is root.

Contents – Coils of jejunum and ileum
- Superior mesenteric artery
- Superior mesenteric vein
- Fat
- Lacteals — lymph vessel of villus.

5. **Supports of uterus:**

Ans. 1. Pelvic diaphragm — by Levator ani and Coccygeus muscle
2. Perineal body — insertion of Levator ani
3. Urogenital diaphragm
4. Transverse cervical ligaments called Mackenrodt's ligament

   Fixes the cervix
5. Round ligament of uterus
6. Anteverted and anteflexed position of uterus
7. Broad ligaments of uterus
8. Uterovesical fold of peritoneum
9. Rectouterine fold of peritoneum.

6. **Positions of uterus:**

Ans. Anteversion and anteflexion

Anteflexion – long axis of body

+

long axis of cervix

make angle of 120 degree

Anteversion – long axis of body

+

long axis of vagina

angle is 90 degree

Normal uterus is in anteversion and anteflexion position.

7. Various positions of appendix:

Ans. 12 o'clock – Retrocaecal

11 o'clock – Paracolic

Splenic – 2 o'clock

Pelvic – 4 o'clock

Midinguinal or 6 o'clock

Commonest position is 12 o'clock in 65% cases.

Next – pelvic, i.e. 4 o'clock

Shown in relation with hands of clock

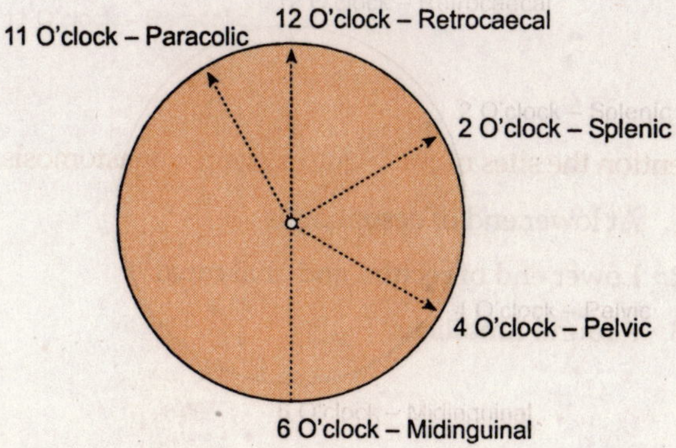

8. What is MacBurney's point ? What is its importance ? What is referred pain of appendicitis ?

Ans. Draw the line on anterior abdominal wall connecting anterior superior iliac spine with umbilicus.

Junction of medial 2/3 and lateral 1/3 the point is called MacBurney's point.

Important: This is site of maximum tenderness in acute appendicitis. Appendix has nerve supply from T10 segment of spinal cord. Also same to the skin around umbilicus, so pain of acute appendicitis is first felt around umbilicus. This is called referred pain of acute appendicitis.

Mac Burney's point on anterior abdominal wall

(Right side)

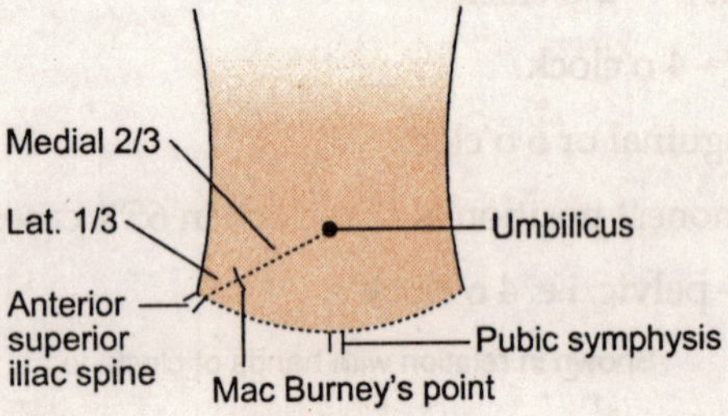

9. Mention the sites of portal and systemic anastomosis.

Ans. 1. At lower end of oesophagus

2. Lower end of rectum and anal canal

3. Around umbilicus

4. Bare area of liver — triangular area on posterior surface of right lobe of liver and this is in between two layers of coronary ligament
5. Posterior abdominal wall.

10. Branches of superior mesenteric artery:

Ans. This is the unpaired branch of abdominal aorta and arises at L1 vertebral level. Called midgut artery branches are:

1. Jejunal
2. Ileal
3. Inferior pancreaticoduodenal artery
4. Right colic
5. Middle colic
6. Iliocolic – gives 4 branches:

   a. Ileal, b. Caecal, c. Colic, d. Appendicular

11. Give the functions of spleen. Name the conditions in which spleen is enlarged. Name the structures in hilum.

Ans. Spleen has following functions:

1. It is the organ which produces immunity as it is the largest organ of lymphoid tissue.
2. It is the organ of reticuloendothelial system, so destroys RBC who have completed their lifespan of 120 days.

Conditions where the spleen is enlarged:

Enlargement of spleen is splenomegaly.

In 1. Typhoid

2. Malaria
3. Kala-azar

Structures in hilum of spleen:

1. Tail of pancreas
2. Branches of splenic artery
3. Tributaries of splenic vein

These 3 structures are surrounded by lienorenal ligament.

Structures in hilum of spleen

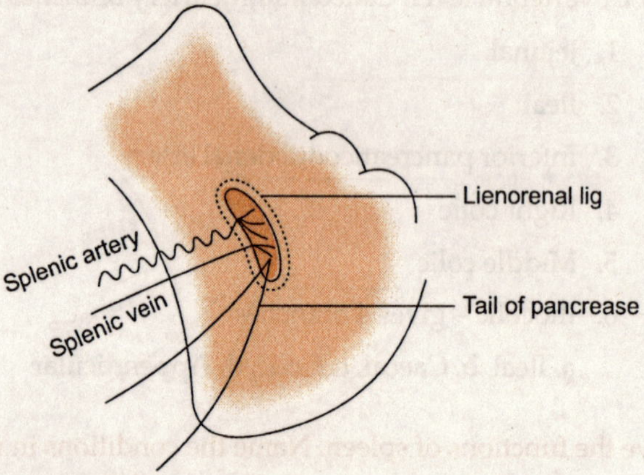

12. Enumerate the paired branches of abdominal aorta.

Ans. 1. Inferior phrenic arteries
2. Middle suprarenal arteries
3. Renal arteries
4. Testicular or ovarian arteries
5. Four lumbar arteries
   – from dorsal side
6. Common iliac.

13. Enumerate unpaired branches of abdominal aorta.

Ans. 1. Coeliac artery – called foregut artery

2. Superior mesenteric artery
   – called midgut artery
3. Inferior mesenteric artery
   – called hindgut artery
4. Median sacral artery.

14. Name the ligaments of liver.

Ans. 1. Flaciform ligament — liver is connected with anterior abdominal wall
2. Ligamentum teres — it is obliterated left umbilical vein
3. Right triangular ligament — superior surface of right lobe with diaphragm
4. Left triangular ligament — superior surface of left lobe with diaphragm
5. Coronary ligament — liver connected with posterior abdominal wall.
6. Ligamentum venosum — it is ductus venosus

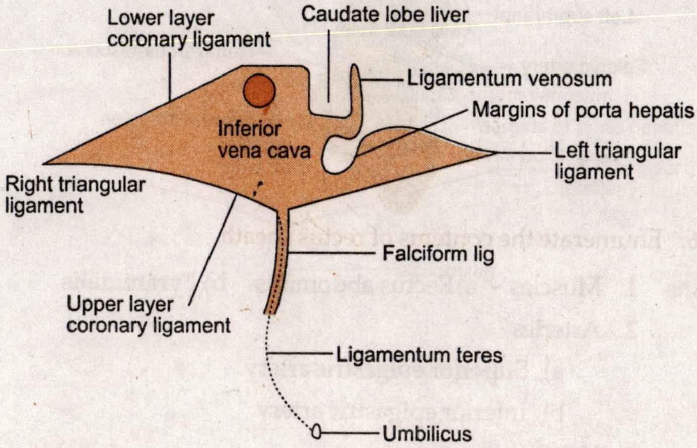

7. Lesser omentum — from margins of porta hepatis to hepatogastric part.
   a) Lesser curvature of stomach — hepatoduodenal
   b) First one inch of duodenum.

15. Name the structures of stomach bed.

Ans. 1. Left crus of diaphragm
2. Left kidney
3. Left suprarenal gland
4. Body of pancreas
5. Transverse colon
6. Transverse mesocolon
7. Spleen
8. Splenic artery
9. Lesser sac.

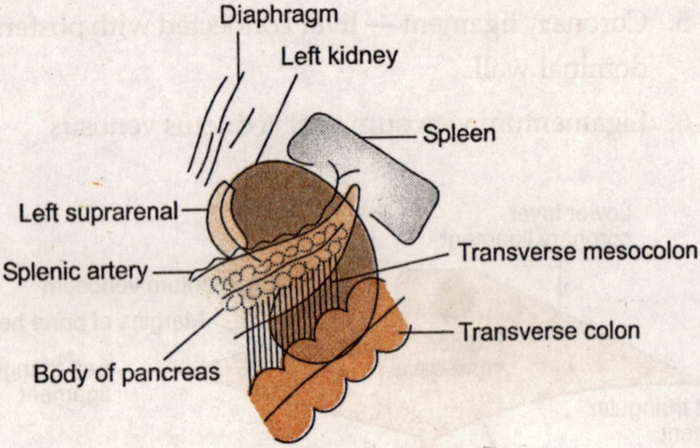

16. Enumerate the contents of rectus sheath.

Ans. 1. Muscles – a) Rectus abdominis b) Pyramidalis
2. Arteries
   a) Superior epigastric artery
   b) Inferior epigastric artery
3. Veins

4. Lower five intercostal nerves

+

Subcostal nerve

17. Name the capsules of kidney.

Ans. 1. Fibrous capsule lies in contact with the kidney

2. Fat — called perirenal fat or perinephric fat or perinephric

If this fat reduces in amount kidney moves from its position, it is called mobile kidney

3. Renal fascia

Remember (3F)

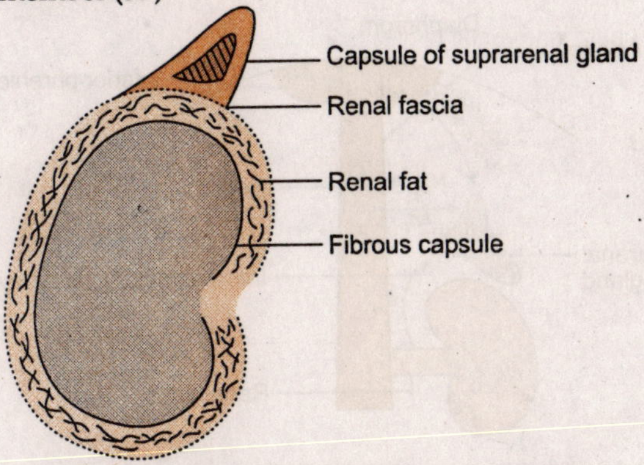

Diagram of kidney showing 3 capsules.

18. Give the blood supply of suprarenal gland.

Ans. Arteries:

1. Superior suprarenal arteries

↓

Branch of inferior phrenic artery

↓

Inferior phrenic — are paired branches of abdominal aorta

2. Middle suprarenal arteries from abdominal aorta
3. Inferior suprarenal arteries from renal arteries

Arteries enter the gland at its periphery.

Vein:

Only one vein:

Right suprarenal vein drains the gland and joins with inferior vena cava.

Left suprarenal vein join with left renal vein.

The point from where vein comes out is called hilum of suprarenal gland.

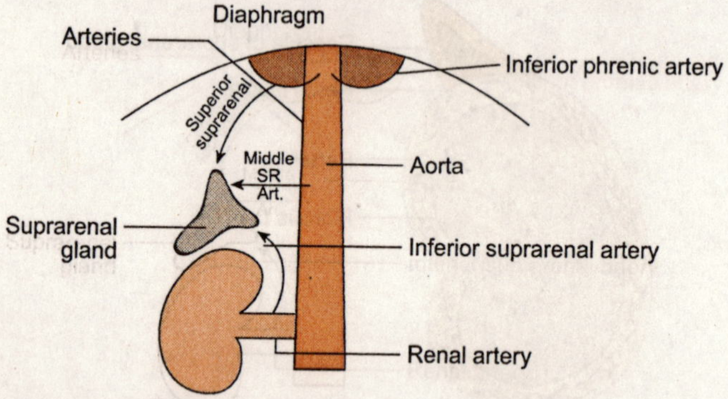

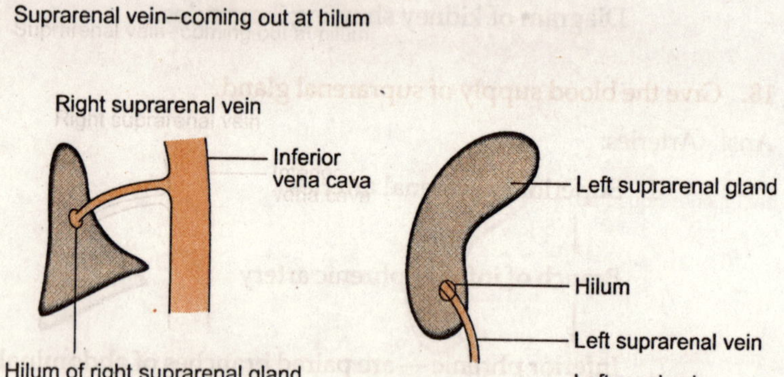

19. Name the vascular segments of kidney.

Ans. Anteriorly:

1. Apical
2. Upper
3. Middle
4. Lower

Posteriorly:

5. Posterior

Total number of five vascular segments.

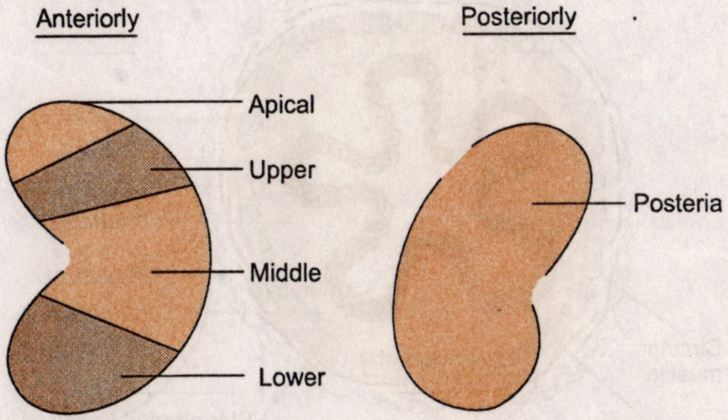

20. What are constrictions of ureter ? Give the histology and development.

Ans. Ureter shows three constrictions — when catheterisation is needed. These constrictions are noted

- first — at pelviureteric junction
- second — at brim of pelvis
- third — where it opens in urinary bladder

Histology

1. Outer peritoneal coat

2. Involuntary muscle coat
   - outer circular
   - inner longitudinal
3. Submucosa — lies in blood vessels, nerves
4. Mucosa — shows longitudinal and temporary folds

Because of the longitudinal folds, the lumen is star-shaped.

Mucosal folds are lined by transitional epithelium.

Histology of ureter

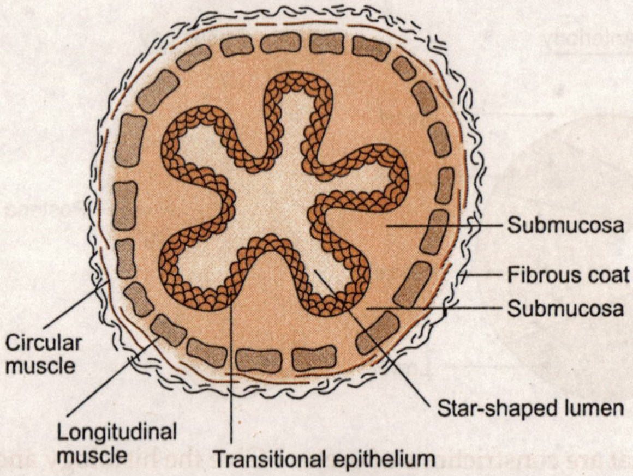

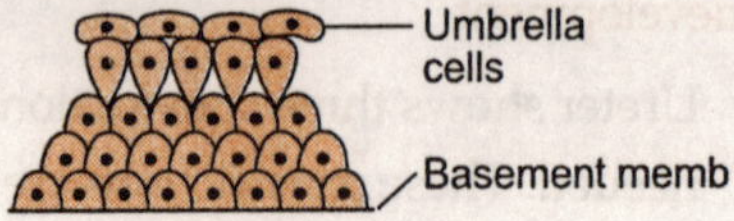

Develops from ureteric bud, which arises from mesonephric duct.

21. Draw the interior of anal canal.

Ans.

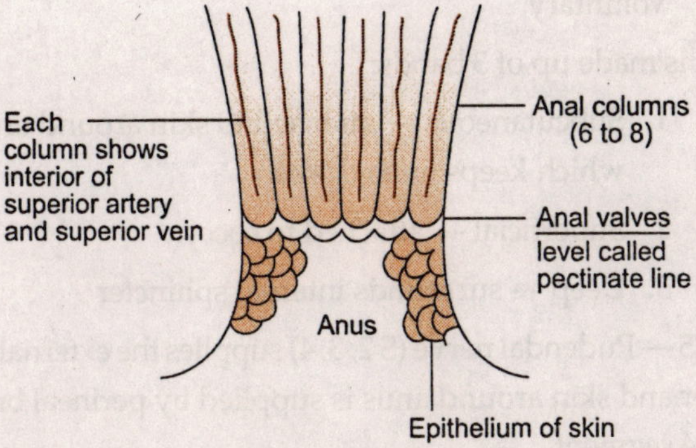

Upper 2/3 of interior of anal canal shows 6 to 8 vertical folds called anal columns. Each anal column contains the branch of superior renal artery and vein.

At the lower end of anal column — duplication of mucus membrane called anal valves. The level of valves is pectinate line.

Above pectinate line — the anal canal is endodermal and lined by columnar epithelium.

Below pectinate line — anal canal is ectodermal and lined by skin.

22. Sphincters of anal canal:

Ans. The length of anal canal is 3.5 to 4 cm.

Upper 2/3 is having internal sphincter — involuntary.

It is the circular muscle coat of rectum continues as internal sphincter.

Supplied by autonomic nerves.

Entire anal canal is surrounded by external sphincter

↓

Voluntary

It is made up of 3 bands:

1. Subcutaneous — attached to skin around anus which keeps anus closed
2. Superficial — attached to coccyx
3. Deep — surrounds internal sphincter

4.5 — Pudendal nerve (S 2, 3, 4) supplies the external sphincter and skin around anus is supplied by perineal branch of S 4 segment.

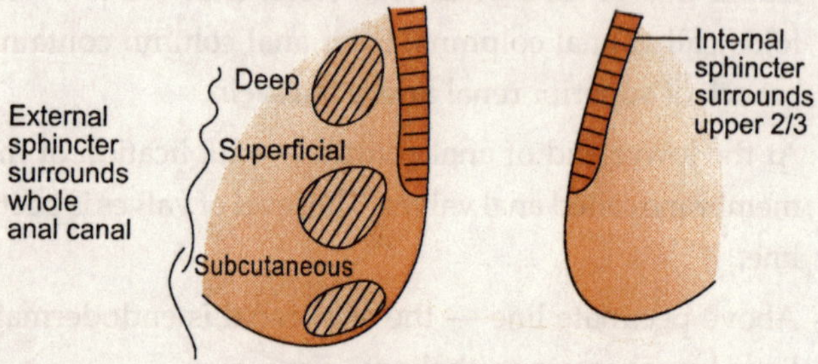

23. Draw the diagram of base of urinary bladder in males.

Ans. Base is the posterior surface of the urinary bladder.

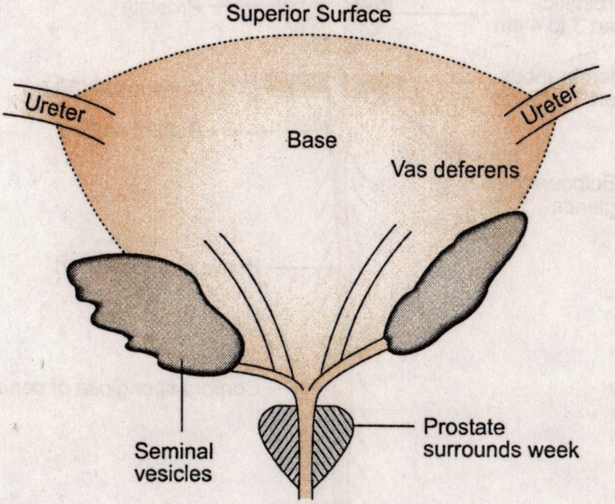

Related to – Seminal vesicles

– Vas deferens.

24. Show the parts of male urethra.

Ans. Starts at internal urethral orifice which lies at neck of urinary bladder and ends at external urethral orifice.

Parts — total length of male urethra is 18 cm

Prostatic part — 3 to 4 cm

First 4 cm part is surrounded by prostate, so called prostatic part.

– 1 to 2 cm is membranous part 1 to 2 cm

– Penile part or spongy 13 to 14 cm part.

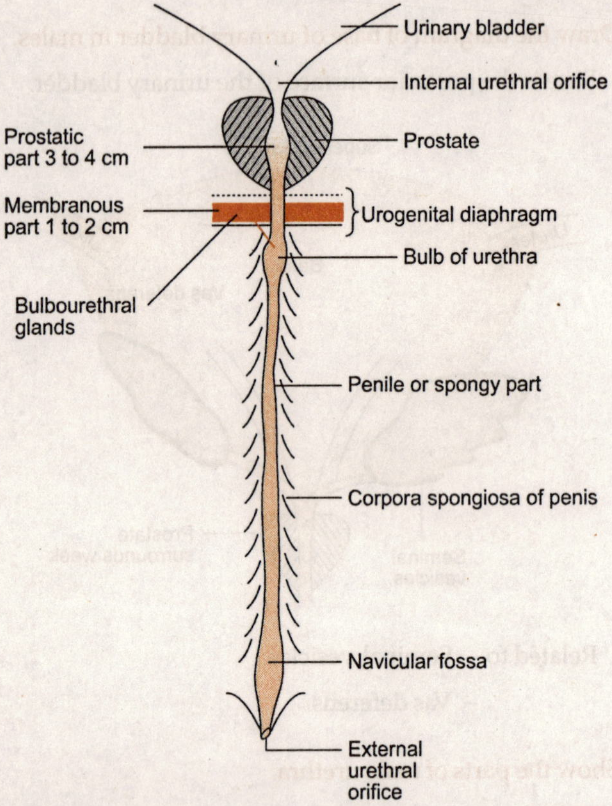

25. Ischiorectal fossa and contents:

Ans. Triangular space between

- Ischial tuberosity laterally
- Rectum and anal canal medially

Contents:

1. Pad of fat called ischiorectal pad of fat
2. Inferior rectal vessels and nerves
3. Perineal branch of S 4 segment

4. Lies in lateral wall — Alcock's canal *or* pudendal canal

This contains pudendal nerve and internal pudendal artery.

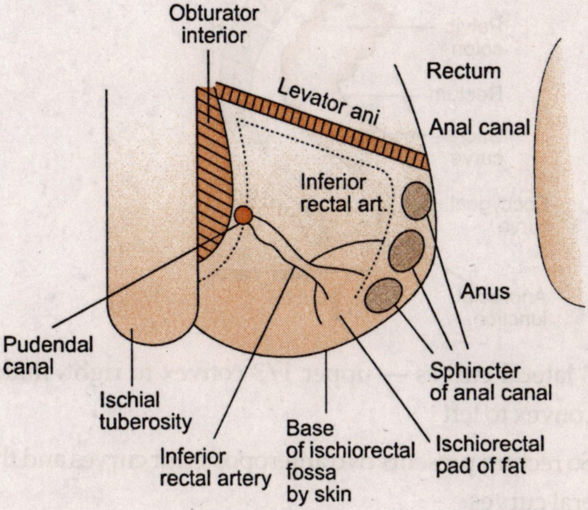

Diagram showing ischiorectal fossa.

26. What are curves of rectum ?

Ans. Anteroposterior curves – Rectum follows concavity of sacrum — it is sacral or pelvic curve

– Rectum follows convexity of coccyx — it is called coccygeal or perineal curve

Diagram — anteroposterior curves

Curves of rectum Anteroposterior ② — Sacral curve or pelvic curve; Coccygeal curve or perineal curve

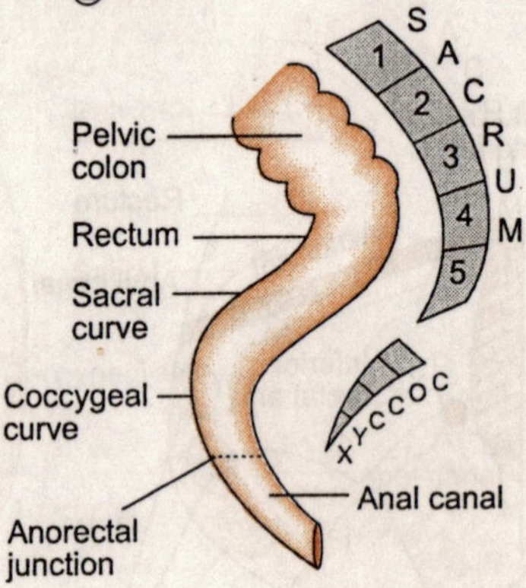

3 lateral curves — upper 1/3 convex to right, middle 1/3 convex to left

So rectum presents two anteroposterior curves and three lateral curves.

Lateral curves –③

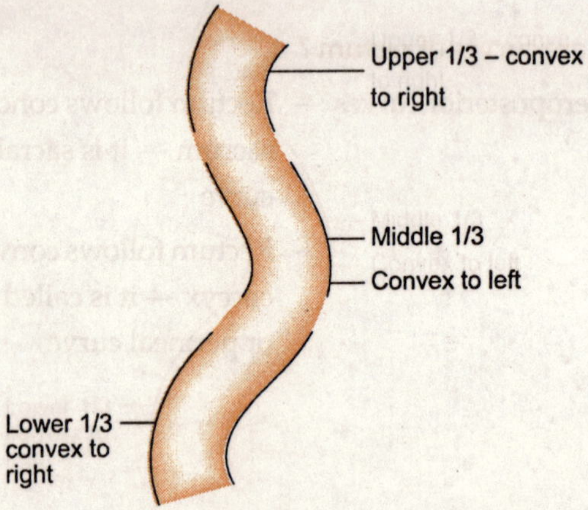

Chapter 8: Head, Neck and Face

Multiple Choice Questions

1) Coronal suture is the:
   a. Plane synovial joint
   b. Primary cartilaginous joint
   c. Fibrous joint
   d. Secondary cartilaginous joint

2) Pterion on norma lateralis shows H-shaped union of:
   a. Frontal bone, parietal bone, temporal bone and greater wing of sphenoid bone
   b. Frontal bone, temporal bone, zygomatic and sphenoid bone
   c. Greater wing of sphenoid, frontal, occipital and parietal bone
   d. None of the above

3) Deep to pterion lies:
   a. Anterior division of middle meningeal artery
   b. Middle meningeal vein
   c. Stem of lateral sulcus
   d. All of the above

Ans. 1. c 2. a 3. d

4) Following bone develops in the second year:

a. Mastoid process of temporal bone

b. Styloid process of temporal bone

c. Ramus of mandible

d. Petrous part of temporal bone

5) Anterior fontanelle closes at the age of:

a. 6 months b. 9 months

c. 12 months d. 18 months

6) Posterior fontanelle closes at the age of:

a. 3 to 6 months b. After 6 months

c. At 12th month d. Just after birth

7) Jugular foramen at base of skull transmits following nerves *except*:

a. Glossopharyngeal nerve

b. Fascial nerve

c. Vagus nerve

d. Accessory nerve

8) Joint between condyles of occipital bone and atlas vertebra is:

a. Synovial — ball and socket

b. Synovial — condyloid

c. Synovial — pivot

d. Synovial — ellipsoid

Ans. 4. a 5. d 6. a 7. b 8. b

9) Following bone is the pneumatic bone:

a. Maxilla
b. Mandible
c. Occipital
d. Petrous part of temporal bone

10) Optic foramen transmits:

a. Optic nerve
b. Ophthalmic artery
c. a + b
d. Ophthalmic veins

11) Through superior orbital fissure passes following structures *except*:

a. Oculomotor nerve
b. Abducent nerve
c. Optic nerve
d. Ophthalmic nerve branch of trigeminal nerve

12) Nerve coming out through stylomastoid foramen is:

a. Glossopharyngeal nerve
b. Vestibulocochlear nerve
c. Vagus nerve
d. Facial nerve

13) Through foramen magnum passes following structures *except*:

a. Medulla oblongata with meninges
b. Vertebral arteries
c. Anterior and posterior spinal arteries
d. Cranial part of accessory nerve

Ans. 9. a 10. c 11. c 12. d 13. d

14) Following joint is pivot joint:

a. Atlantoaxial (median)

b. Atlantooccipital

c. Temporomandibular

d. None of the above

15) Foramen transversarium is the characteristic feature of:

a. Thoracic vertebrae

b. Cervical vertebrae

c. Lumbar vertebrae

d. All of the above

16) Through foramen transversarium passes:

a. Vertebral artery   b. Vertebral vein

c. a + b   d. Corresponding spinal nerve

17) In between laminae of the vertebrae lies:

a. Ligamentum nuchae

b. Ligamentum flavum

c. Ligamentum denticulatum

d. None of the above

18) Following ligament contains yellow elastic fibres:

a. Ligamentum flavum

b. Ligaments of auditory ossicles

c. a + b

d. None of the above

Ans. 14. a 15. b 16. c 17. b 18. a

19) Total number of vertebrae in vertebral column is:

a. Thirty one b. Thirty
c. Thirty two d. Thirty three

20) Joint between the bodies of vertebrae is:

a. Primary cartilaginous joint
b. Secondary cartilaginous joint
c. Fibrous joint
d. Plane synovial joint

21) Cervical curve of vertebral column develops at the age of:

a. 6 months after birth b. Just after birth
c. In second year d. 18 months

22) Vertebra prominence is:

a. Atlas
b. Axis
c. Seventh cervical vertebra
d. None of the above

23) Crista galli is the part of:

a. Sphenoid bone b. Ethmoid bone
c. Frontal bone d. Temporal bone

24) Superciliary arches indicate the position of:

a. Frontal air sinus b. Ethmoidal air sinus
c. Sphenoidal air sinus d. None of the above

Ans. 19. d 20. b 21. a 22. c 23. b 24. a

25) Following bone is the unpaired bone of skull:

a. Maxilla b. Temporal

c. Occipital d. Parietal

26) Gomphosis is:

a. Fibrous joint

b. Plane synovial joint

c. Primary cartilaginous joint

d. Secondary cartilaginous joint

27) Styloid apparatus is formed by:

a. Styloid process of temporal bone

b. Stylomandibular and stylohyoid ligaments

c. Styloglossus, Stylohyoid and Stylopharyngeus muscle

d. All of the above

28) Occipitofrontalis muscle shows:

a. Insertion on epicranial aponeurosis

b. Supplied by facial nerve

c. Second arch muscle

d. All of the above

29) Dangerous zone of scalp is:

a. Second layer

b. Third layer

c. Fourth layer – zone of loose connective tissue

d. Beneath pericranium

Ans. 25. c 26. a 27. d 28. d 29. c

30) Following vein show no valves:

a. Dural venous sinuses
b. Emissary veins
c. a + b
d. None of the above

31) Following muscles form floor of posterior triangle *except*:

a. Splenius capitis
b. Semispinalis capitis
c. Levator scapulae
d. Sternocleidomastoid muscle

32) Spinal part of accessory nerve shows all features *except*:

a. Supplies Trapezius and Sternocleidomastoid muscle
b. Ascends through foramen magnum
c. Originates from nucleus ambiguous
d. Originates from C 1, C 2, C 3, C 4, C 5 segments of spinal cord

33) Air embolus is commonly with:

a. External jugular vein
b. Internal jugular vein
c. Anterior jugular vein
d. Facial vein

34) Anterior belly of Digastric muscle is supplied by:

a. Facial nerve
b. Maxillary nerve
c. Mandibular nerve
d. Ansa cervicalis

Ans. 30. c 31. d 32. c 33. a 34. c

35) Digastric triangle contains *except*:

a. Submandibular salivary gland — superficial part

b. Submandibular salivary gland — deep part

c. Submandibular lymph nodes

d. Facial artery and facial vein

36) External carotid artery gives following branches *except*:

a. Superior thyroid artery

b. Inferior thyroid artery

c. Facial artery

d. Occipital artery

37) Following structures are enclosed by carotid sheath:

a. Carotid artery
b. Internal jugular vein
c. Vagus nerve
d. All of the above

38) Following muscle is supplied by glossopharyngeal nerve:

a. Styloglossus
b. Stylohyoid
c. Stylopharyngeus
d. Sternocleidomastoid

39) Following nerves form ansa cervicalis:

a. Hypoglossal nerve

b. C 1 segment of spinal cord

c. C 2, 3 segments of spinal cord

d. All of the above

Ans. 35. b 36. b 37. d 38. c 39. d

40) Following muscle is supplied by facial nerve:

a. Anterior belly of Digastric

b. Posterior belly of Digastric

c. Stapedius muscle of middle ear

d. b + c

41) Following muscles are Infrahyoid muscles:

a. Sternohyoid

b. Sternothyroid

c. Thyrohyoid, Omohyoid

d. All of the above

42) Cricoid cartilage shows:

a. Lies at the level of 6th cervical vertebra

b. Only complete cartilage in the wall of larynx

c. Example of hyaline cartilage

d. All of the above

43) Stylomandibular ligament is:

a. Thick band of investing layer of cervical fascia

b. Attached to angle of mandible

c. Separates parotid and submandibular salivary gland

d. All of the above

44) Sibson's fascia or suprapleural membrane is derived from:

a. Prevertebral layer of cervical fascia

b. Investing layer of deep cervical fascia

c. Pretracheal fascia

d. None of the above

Ans. 40. d 41. d 42. d 43. d 44. a

45) Skin over parotid gland is supplied by:

a. Trigeminal nerve
b. Great auricular nerve
c. Facial nerve
d. None of the above

46) Orbicularis oculi muscle:

a. Closes the eye
b. Supplied by facial nerve
c. Spreads lacrimal fluid over whole eye
d. All of the above

47) Greater petrosal nerve arises from:

a. Glossopharyngeal nerve
b. Facial nerve
c. Vagus nerve
d. None of the above

48) Parotid capsule is formed by:

a. Investing layer of cervical fascia
b. Pretracheal layer
c. Prevertebral layer
d. None of the above

49) Superior sagittal sinus continues as:

a. Left transverse sinus
b. Right transverse sinus
c. Straight sinus
d. Sigmoid sinus

Ans. 45. b 46. d 47. b 48. a 49. b

50) Along lesser wing of sphenoid bone lies:

a. Superior petrosal sinus
b. Sphenoparietal sinus
c. Inferior petrosal sinus
d. None of the above

51) Straight sinus is formed by the union of:

a. Superior sagittal sinus and great cerebral vein
b. Superior sagittal sinus and inferior sagittal sinus
c. Inferior sagittal sinus and great cerebral vein
d. Great cerebral vein and middle cerebral vein

52) Transverse sinus continues as:

a. Sigmoid sinus
b. Sphenoparietal sinus
c. Superior petrosal sinus
d. None of the above

53) Sigmoid sinus continues as:

a. External jugular vein
b. Internal jugular vein
c. Anterior jugular vein
d. None of the above

54) Ophthalmic veins open in:

a. Cavernous sinus
b. Sphenoparietal sinus
c. Superior sagittal sinus
d. Inferior sagittal sinus

55) Cavernous sinus contains following nerves *except*:

a. Mandibular nerve
b. Abducent nerve
c. Trochlear nerve
d. Maxillary nerve

Ans. 50. b 51. c 52. a 53. b 54. a 55. a

56) Dural venous sinuses have following features *except*:

a. No valves

b. Lined by endothelium

c. Drain the brain and meninges

d. Having smooth muscle in the walls

57) Confluence of sinus is the point at:

a. External occipital protuberance

b. Internal occipital protuberance

c. Slightly right to internal occipital protuberance

d. Slightly left to internal occipital protuberance

58) Adenohypophysis has following features:

a. Develops from Rathke's pouch

b. It is large anterior part of gland

c. Made up of chromophobe cells and chromophil cells

d. All of the above

59) Rathke's pouch is:

a. Ectodermal b. Endodermal

c. a + b d. Mesodermal

60) Infundibulum is the part of:

a. Neurohypophysis

b. Adenohypophysis

c. Pars intermedius

d. None of the above

Ans. 56. d 57. c 58. d 59. a 60. a

61) Ophthalmic nerve gives following branches *except*:

a. Frontal
b. Nasociliary
c. Lacrimal
d. Infraorbital

62) Following muscle is not supplied by mandibular nerve:

a. Posterior belly of Digastric
b. Anterior belly of Digastric
c. Tensor palati
d. Mylohyoid

63) Thymus shows following facts *except*:

a. Form T lymphocytes
b. Develops from third pharyngeal pouch
c. Microscopically shows Hassall's corpuscles
d. Reduces in weight before puberty

64) Pretracheal fascia forms capsule for:

a. Parotid gland
b. Thyroid gland
c. Submandibular gland
d. Parathyroid gland

65) Thyroid gland has its isthmus covering:

a. Second, third, fourth tracheal rings
b. Second and third tracheal rings
c. Third and fourth tracheal rings
d. Third, fourth and fifth tracheal rings

Ans. 61. d 62. a 63. d 64. b 65. a

66) Thyroid gland develops from:

a. Second pharyngeal pouch

b. Median thyroid diverticulum

c. Rathke's pouch

d. None of the above

67) Parafollicular cells of thyroid develop from:

a. Second pharyngeal pouch

b. Median thyroid diverticulum

c. Ultimobranchial bodies

d. Third pharyngeal pouch

68) Blood supply of the thyroid is derived from:

a. Pair of superior thyroid artery

b. Pair of inferior thyroid artery

c. Thyroid-ima-artery

d. All of the above

69) Median thyroid diverticulum is:

a. Ectodermal b. Mesodermal

c. Endodermal d. Ectodermal and endodermal

70) Thyroid follicles are lined by:

a. Simple cuboidal epithelium in its moderate activity

b. Simple columnar epithelium

c. Simple squamous epithelium

d. None of the above

Ans. 66. b 67. c 68. d 69. c 70. a

71) Pale cells or clear cells are:

a. Follicular cells
b. Parafollicular cells
c. a + b
d. None of the above

72) Parathyroid III is:

a. Superior parathyroid
b. Inferior parathyroid
c. a + b
d. None

73) Fourth pharyngeal pouch forms:

a. Superior parathyroids
b. Inferior parathyroids
c. a + b
d. None of the above

74) Trachea shows following facts:

a. Starts at C 6 level
b. Wall shows horse-shoe shaped rings of hyaline cartilages
c. Lined by pseudostratified columnar ciliated epithelium
d. All of the above

75) Trachea divides at:

a. T 3 level
b. T 4 level
c. T 5 level
d. None of the above

76) Glossopharyngeal nerve gives following branch:

a. Greater petrosal nerve
b. Lesser petrosal nerve
c. Deep petrosal nerve
d. None of the above

Ans. 71. b 72. b 73. a 74. d 75. b 76. b

77) Third arch nerve is:

a. Mandibular nerve b. Facial nerve

c. Vagus nerve d. Glossopharyngeal nerve

78) All the muscles of face are supplied by facial nerve *except*:

a. Orbicularis oculi

b. Levator palpebrae superioris

c. Buccinator

d. Orbicularis oris

79) Investing layer of cervical fascia encloses:

a. Sternocleidomastoid and Trapezius

b. Parotid and submandibular gland muscle

c. Form stylomandibular ligament

d. All of the above

80) Following is the branch of facial nerve:

a. Chorda tympani nerve

b. Lesser petrosal nerve

c. Tympanic nerve

d. None of the above

81) Dangerous zone of face is:

a. Area around upper lip b. Area of chin

c. Area of lower lip d. Forehead region

Ans. 77. d 78. b 79. d 80. a 81. a

82) Following are the muscles of mastication *except*:

a. Masseter

b. Temporalis

c. Buccinator

d. Lateral and Medial pterygoid muscles

83) All the muscles of mastication are supplied by:

a. Mandibular nerve

b. Hypoglossal nerve

c. Glossopharyngeal nerve

d. Maxillary nerve

84) The only muscle which depresses the mandible is:

a. Masseter muscle

b. Lateral pterygoid muscle

c. Temporalis muscle

d. Medial pterygoid muscle

85) Temporomandibular joint is:

a. Synovial — ball and socket variety

b. Synovial — condyloid

c. Synovial — pivot

d. Secondary cartilaginous joint

86) Transverse facial artery arises from:

a. External carotid artery

b. Facial artery

c. Maxillary artery

d. Superficial temporal artery

Ans. 82. c 83. a 84. b 85. b 86. d

87) Secretomotor nerve supply of parotid gland passes through:

a. Otic ganglion
b. Submandibular ganglion
c. Pterygopalatine ganglion
d. None of the above

88) Parotid gland contains:

a. Facial nerve
b. Retromandibular vein
c. End of external carotid artery
d. All of the above

89) Following gland is ectodermal in origin:

a. Thyroid gland
b. Parotid gland
c. Submandibular salivary gland
d. Sublingual salivary gland

90) Nasolacrimal duct opens in:

a. Superior meatus of nose
b. Middle meatus of nose
c. Inferior meatus of nose
d. Nasopharynx

Ans. 87. a 88. d 89. b 90. c

91) Trochlear nerve supplies:

a. Superior rectus of eye
b. Superior oblique of eye
c. Lateral rectus of eye
d. Medial rectus of eye

92) Abducent nerve supplies:

a. Lateral rectus
b. Medial rectus
c. Superior rectus
d. Inferior rectus

93) Oculomotor nerve supplies:

a. Levator palpebrae superioris muscle
b. Superior rectus muscle
c. Inferior rectus muscle
d. All of the above

94) Optic nerve is formed by axons of:

a. Rod + Cone cells
b. Bipolar cells
c. Ganglion cells
d. None of the above

95) Secretomotor nerve supply of the lacrimal gland passes through:

a. Otic ganglion
b. Pterygopalatine ganglion *or* sphenopalatine
c. Ciliary ganglion
d. None of the above

Note: Pterygopalatine ganglion is also called sphenopalatine ganglion

Ans. 91. b 92. a 93. d 94. c 95. b

96) Lacrimal glands are:

a. Ectodermal in origin b. Mesodermal

c. Endodermal d. a + b

97) If the person is unable to move the eye downwards and laterally, the nerve injured is:

a. Oculomotor b. Trochlear

c. Abducent d. Ophthalmic

98) Ptosis is due to paralysis of:

a. Superior rectus

b. Lavator palpebrae superioris

c. Both of the above

d. None of the above

99) Ciliary ganglion is connected with:

a. Optic nerve b. Oculomotor nerve

c. Ophthalmic nerve d. b + c

100) Sphincter pupillae and Ciliaris muscle are supplied by:

a. Oculomotor nerve b. Abducent nerve

c. Trochlear nerve d. None of the above

101) Loss of accommodation is paralysis of:

a. Ciliaris muscle

b. Superior and inferior obliques

c. Sphincter pupillae

d. Dilator pupillae

Ans. 96. a 97. b 98. b 99. d 100. a 101. a

102) Cells of retina responsible for colour vision:

a. Rods
b. Cones
c. Both of the above
d. None of the above

103) Cornea is lined by:

a. Stratified squamous moist epithelium
b. Stratified columnar epithelium
c. Stratified squamous dry variety
d. None of the above

104) Secretion of lacrimal gland is:

a. Serous
b. Mucus
c. Oily
d. Seromucous

105) Through foramen ovale pauses:

a. Mandibular nerve
b. Lesser petrosal nerve
c. Accessory meningeal artery
d. Emissary vein
e. All of the above

106) Ligament of first arch is:

a. Stylohyoid ligament
b. Sphenomandibular ligament
c. Stylomandibular ligament
d. None of the above

Ans. 102. b 103. a 104. a 105. e 106. b

107) Mandibular foramen transmits:

a. Inferior alveolar nerve
b. Inferior alveolar vessels
c. Both of the above
d. None of the above

108) Skin over angle of mandible is supplied by:

a. Mandibular nerve
b. Facial nerve
c. Great auricular nerve
d. None of the above

109) Through foramen spinosum passes:

a. Meningeal branch of mandibular nerve *or* nervous spinosus
b. Middle meningeal artery
c. a + b
d. None of the above

110) Middle meningeal artery arises from:

a. Vertebral artery
b. Internal carotid artery
c. Maxillary artery
d. Superficial temporal artery

111) Nerve to Medial pterygoid muscle supplies:

a. Medial pterygoid muscle
b. Tensor tympani muscle
c. Tensor palati muscle
d. All of the above

Ans. 107. c 108. c 109. c 110. c 111. d

112) Lingual nerve arises from:

a. Trunk of mandibular nerve

b. Anterior division of mandibular nerve

c. Posterior division of mandibular nerve

d. Hypoglossal nerve

113) Otic ganglion is connected with:

a. Maxillary nerve
b. Glossopharyngeal nerve

c. Mandibular nerve
d. b + c

114) Chorda tympani branch of the facial nerve supplies through:

a. Lingual branch of mandibular nerve

b. Inferior alveolar nerve

c. Auriculotemporal nerve

d. Buccal branch

115) Following nerve arises from posterior division of mandibular nerve:

a. Nerve to Medial pterygoid

b. Branch to Masseter

c. Buccal nerve

d. Auriculotemporal nerve

116) Preganglionic nerve for otic ganglion is:

a. Greater petrosal nerve of 7th

b. Lesser petrosal nerve of 9th

c. Auriculotemporal nerve of mandibular

d. Chorda tympani of 7th

Ans. 112. c 113. d 114. a 115. d 116. b

117) Following branch of external carotid artery is having tortuous course:

a. Facial b. Lingual

c. Occipital d. Maxillary

118) Wharton's duct is duct of:

a. Parotid gland b. Sublingual gland

c. Lacrimal gland d. Submandibular gland

119) Stensen's duct is duct of:

a. Thyroid gland b. Parotid gland

c. Submandibular gland d. None of the above

120) Submandibular salivary gland shows following facts *except*:

a. Seromucus gland

b. Wharton's duct open in floor of mouth

c. Lies in digastric triangle

d. Secretomotor nerve supply passes through otic ganglion

121) Secretomotor nerve supply to submandibular salivary passes through:

a. Otic ganglion

b. Submandibular ganglion

c. Pterygopalatine ganglion

d. None of the above

Ans. 117. a 118. d 119. b 120. d 121. b

122) Auditory tube opens in:

a. Oropharynx b. Inferior meatus of nose

c. Nasopharynx d. None of the above

123) Palatine tonsils shows following facts:

a. Lymphoid masses are on either side of oropharynx

b. Develops from second pharyngeal pouch

c. Microscopically crypts are lined by stratified squamous moist-epithelium

d. All of the above

124) Waldeyer's ring is formed by:

a. Lingual tonsils

b. Palatine tonsils

c. Pharyngeal and tubal tonsils

d. All of the above

125) In the tonsillectomy operation source of bleeding is following vessel:

a. Tonsillar artery b. Lingual artery

c. Facial artery d. Paratonsillar vein

126) All the muscles of soft palate are supplied by accessory nerve (cranial part) *except*:

a. Tensor palati b. Levator palati

c. Palatoglossus glossus d. Palatopharyngeus

Ans. 122. c 123. d 124. d 125. d 126. a

127) Tensor palati muscle is supplied by:

a. Glossopharyngeal nerve

b. Mandibular nerve

c. Cranial root of accessory

d. Spinal root of accessory

128) Nasal septum is:

a. Bony
b. Cartilaginous
c. Osseo-cartilaginous
d. Fibrous

129) Bones forming nasal septum are:

a. Vomer

b. Perpendicular plate of ethmoid bone

c. Both of the above

d. None of the above

130) Nasal septum lies in:

a. Midline
b. Slightly to right
c. Slightly to left
d. None of the above

131) Following are the components of nasal septum *except*:

a. Perpendicular plate of ethmoid bone

b. Vomer

c. Septal cartilage

d. Crista galli part of ethmoid bone

Ans. 127. b 128. c 129. c 130. b 131. d

132) Paranasal sinuses perform following functions *except*:

a. Exchange of gases
b. Lighten the weight of skull
c. Resonate the voice
d. Warming of inhaled air

133) Largest bone in lateral wall of nose is:

a. Superior nasal conchus
b. Inferior nasal conchus
c. Middle nasal conchus
d. None of the above

134) Superior meatus shows opening of:

a. Maxillary air sinus
b. Anterior ethmoidal sinus
c. Posterior ethmoidal sinus
d. Middle ethmoidal sinus

135) Maxillary paranasal sinus shows following facts:

a. First sinus to develop
b. Opens in middle meatus of nose
c. Called sinus of Highmore
d. All of the above

Ans. 132. a 133. b 134. c 135. d

136) Secondary reservoir for frontal air sinus is:

a. Maxillary air sinus

b. Anterior ethmoidal sinuses

c. Middle ethmoidal sinuses

d. Posterior ethmoidal sinuses

137) Openings in middle meatus are:

a. Frontal air sinus

b. Maxillary air sinus

c. Anterior and middle ethmoidal sinuses

d. All of the above

138) In the sphenoethmoidal recess opens:

a. Sphenoidal air sinus

b. Anterior ethmoidal sinuses

c. Middle ethmoidal sinuses

d. Posterior ethmoidal sinuses

139) Cribriform plate of ethmoidal bone transmit:

a. Ophthalmic arteries b. Ophthalmic nerve

c. Olfactory nerves d. None of the above

140) This part of nasal septum is called littles area:

a. Anterosuperior part

b. Anteroinferior part

c. Posterosuperior part

d. Posteroinferior part

Ans. 136. a 137. c 138. a 139. c 140. b

141) Goitre is the enlargement of:

a. Parotids
b. Thyroid gland
c. Parathyroids
d. Submandibular

142) Following nerve is special sensory nerve:

a. Vagus nerve
b. Vestibulocochlear nerve
c. Trigeminal nerve
d. Accessory nerve

143) The branch of vagus which does not arise in neck:

a. Right recurrent laryngeal nerve
b. Left recurrent laryngeal nerve
c. Right superior laryngeal nerve
d. Left superior laryngeal nerve

144) The superior laryngeal nerve arises from:

a. Vagus nerve
b. Hypoglossal nerve
c. Trigeminal nerve
d. None of the above

145) Complete cartilage in the wall of larynx is:

a. Epiglottis
b. Thyroid cartilage
c. Arytenoid cartilage
d. Cricoid cartilage

146) Following is elastic cartilage:

a. Thyroid cartilage
b. Epiglottis
c. Cartilage of ear
d. b + c

Ans. 141. b 142. b 143. b 144. a 145. c 146. d

147) Cricothyroid muscle has following features *except*:

a. Tenses vocal cords
b. Supplied by superior laryngeal nerve
c. Extrinsic muscle of larynx
d. Intrinsic muscle of larynx

148) Sole abductor of vocal cord is:

a. Oblique arytenoid
b. Cricothyroid
c. Posterior cricoarytenoid
d. Transverse arytenoid

149) Cadaveric position of vocal cords is because of injury to:

a. Both side recurrent laryngeal nerves
b. One recurrent laryngeal nerve
c. External laryngeal nerve
d. Internal laryngeal nerve

150) Vocal cords contain following structures *except*:

a. Contains muscle fibres of Vocalis
b. Contains nerves
c. Lined by mucous membrane, i.e. stratified squamous moist
d. Submucosa and blood vessels

Ans. 147. c 148. c 149. a 150. d

151) All the muscles of tongue are supplied by hypoglossal nerve *except*:

a. Hypoglossus muscle
b. Palatoglossus muscle
c. Genioglossus muscle
d. Styloglossus muscle

152) Safety muscle of tongue is:

a. Genioglossus
b. Hypoglossus
c. Styloglossus
d. Palatoglossus

153) All the muscles of tongue develop from:

a. Pre-occipital myotomes
b. Occipital myotomes
c. First arch mesoderm
d. Second arch mesoderm

154) Nerve of taste for anterior 2/3 of tongue is:

a. Chorda tympani of facial nerve
b. Glossopharyngeal nerve
c. Vagus nerve
d. Hypoglossal nerve

155) Nerve of taste for post 1/3 of tongue:

a. Superior laryngeal of vagus
b. Branch of facial nerve
c. Glossopharyngeal nerve
d. None of the above

Ans. 151. b 152. a 153. b 154. a 155. c

156) Circumvallate papillae are innervated by:

a. Glossopharyngeal nerve
b. Facial nerve
c. Vagus nerve
d. Mandibular nerve

157) Tuberculum impar forms:

a. Anterior 1/3 of tongue
b. Anterior 2/3 of tongue
c. Posterior 1/3 of tongue
d. None of the above

158) Mucous membrane of tongue is:

a. Stratified squamous keratinised
b. Stratified squamous nonkeratinised
c. Stratified columnar
d. None of the above

159) Following muscle of tongue is attached to whole length of tongue:

a. Hypoglossus
b. Styloglossus
c. Genioglossus
d. Palatoglossus

160) Lingual tonsils are present in:

a. Posterior 1/3 of tongue
b. Anterior 2/3 of tongue
c. Most posterior part of tongue
d. Oropharynx

Ans. 156. a 157. b 158. b 159. c 160. a

161) Following pharyngeal arches form the tongue *except*:

a. First pharyngeal arch

b. Second pharyngeal arch

c. Third pharyngeal arch

d. Sixth pharyngeal arch

162) Nerve of general sensation for the mucous membrane of anterior 2/3 of tongue is:

a. Chorda tympani of facial

b. Lingual branch of mandibular nerve

c. Glossopharyngeal nerve

d. Vagus nerve

163) Taste buds are absent in:

a. Fungiform papillae

b. Filiform papillae

c. Circumvallate papillae

d. None of the above

164) Ebner's glands are in:

a. Pituitary gland

b. Oesophagus

c. Tongue

d. Epiglottis

165) Change in the shape of tongue is produced by:

a. Extrinsic group of muscles

b. Intrinsic group of muscles

c. Both of the above

d. None of the above

Ans. 161. d 162. b 163. b 164. c 165. b

166) Importance of foramen caecum of tongue:

a. Growth of median thyroid diverticulum

b. Growth of Rathke's pouch

c. Vein passes through it

d. None of the above

167) Stomodeum is:

a. Ectodermal in origin b. Mesodermal

c. Endodermal d. a + b

168) Umbo is in relation with:

a. Auditory ossicles

b. Tympanic membrane

c. Cochlea

d. Vestibule

169) Tensor tympani muscle of middle ear is inserted on:

a. Handle of malleus b. Stapes

c. Incus d. Head of malleus

170) Stapedius of middle ear is supplied by:

a. Mandibular nerve

b. Glossopharyngeal nerve

c. Facial nerve

d. Auricular branch of vagus nerve

Ans. 166. a 167. a 168. b 169. a 170. c

171) Tensor tympani has following features *except*:

a. First arch muscle

b. Supplied by mandibular nerve

c. Inserted on handle of malleus

d. Helps in hearing

172) Joint between malleus and incus is:

a. Synovial— plane

b. Synovial— saddle

c. Synovial condyloid

d. Secondary cartilaginous joint

173) Joint between incus and stapes is:

a. Synovial— ball and socket

b. Primary cartilaginous joint

c. Synovial— plane variety

d. None of the above

174) From Meckel's cartilage of first arch develops:

a. Malleus b. Incus

c. Lingula of mandible d. All of the above

175) Stapes is formed by:

a. First arch cartilage

b. Second arch cartilage

c. Both of the above

d. None of the above

Ans. 171. d 172. b 173. a 174. d 175. b

176) Mastoid air cells lie:

a. Anterior to tympanic cavity
b. Posterior to tympanic cavity
c. Roof of tympanic cavity
d. Floor of tympanic cavity

177) Pharyngeal pouches take part in the formation of tubotympanic recess:

a. Dorsal end of first pharyngeal pouch
b. Dorsal end of second pharyngeal pouch
c. a + b
d. Third pharyngeal pouch

178) Tubotympanic recess forms:

a. Mucous membrane of middle ear
b. Mucous membrane of pharyngotympanic tube
c. Mucous membrane of mastoid air cells
d. All of the above

179) Following statement is not true:

a. Facial nerve supplies post. belly of Digastric muscle
b. Third arch nerve is glossopharyngeal
c. Cricoid cartilage is elastic
d. Hypoglossal nerve supplies all muscles of tongue except Palatoglossus

Ans. 176. b 177. c 178. d 179. c

180) Following arch disappears soon after its formation:

a. Third arch
b. Second arch
c. Fifth arch
d. Fourth arch

181) Hyoid bone is derived from:

a. Second arch
b. Third arch
c. a + b
d. First arch

182) Skull is formed by:

a. Twentyone bones
b. Twentytwo bones
c. Fourteen bones
d. None of the above

183) Bregma is meeting point of:

a. Lamboid suture and sagittal suture
b. Coronal and sagittal suture
c. 4 bones — frontal, parietal, sphenoid, temporal
d. None of the above

184) Through internal acoustic meatus passes following structures *except*:

a. Facial nerve
b. Glossopharyngeal nerve
c. Labyrinthine vessels
d. Vestibulocochlear nerve

185) Posterior triangle contains following nerve:

a. Accessory
b. Vagus
c. Hypoglossal
d. Glossopharyngeal

Ans. 180. c 181. c 182. a 183. b 184. b 185. a

186) Which cranial nerve has no neurilemmal sheath:

a. Optic nerve
b. Oculomotor nerve
c. Trigeminal nerve
d. Vestibulocochlear nerve

187) Falx cerebri is a fold of dura mater contains:

a. Superior sagittal sinus
b. Inferior sagittal sinus
c. Straight sinus
d. All of the above

188) Skeleton of larynx is formed by:

a. Eight cartilages
b. Nine cartilages
c. Ten cartilages
d. None of the above

189) Central artery of reline is branch of:

a. External carotid
b. Ophthalmic artery
c. Anterior cerebral artery
d. None of the above

190) Which is the smallest bone in human body:

a. Phalanges
b. Malleus
c. Incus
d. Stapes

Ans. 186. a 187. d 188. b 189. b 190. d

Short Answer Questions

1. Name the layers of scalp.

Ans. • Skin

- Superficial fascia with blood vessels and nerves and lymphatics
- Epicranial aponeurosis of Occipitofrontalis muscle
- Loose connective tissue
- Pericranium of skull bones, i.e. periosteum covering skull bones

Dangerous zone of scalp — loose connective tissue

2. Which is the dangerous area of face ?

Ans. – Upper lip

– Lower part of nose

3. Give the nerve supply of eyelids.

Ans. Upper eyelid — ophthalmic nerve

Lower eyelid — infraorbital nerve

4. What are parts of lacrimal apparatus ?

Ans. 1. Lacrimal gland and its 10 + 12 slender ducts

2. Conjunctival sac
3. Lacrimal puncta
4. Lacrimal canaliculi
5. Lacrimal sac
6. Nasolacrimal duct

5. Name the extraocular muscles. Give nerve supply.

Ans. 4 – recti – Superior rectus
– Medial rectus
– Inferior rectus
– Lateral rectus

2 – obliques – Superior oblique
– Inferior oblique

Levator palpebrae superioris

Sup – oblique– by trochlear nerve (SO4)

Lal – rectus – by abducent nerve (LR6)

Sup rectus

Medial rectus

Inferior rectus by oculomotor nerve

Infoblique inf-oblique

Levator palpebrae superior

6. Name the openings in middle meatus of nose.

Ans. 1. Opening of frontal air sinus

2. Opening of middle and anterior
+ ethmoidal sinuses

3. Maxillary air sinus

7. Enumerate paranasal air sinuses.

Ans. 1. Frontal

2. Maxillary

3. Ethmoidal – anterior
– middle
– posterior

4. Sphenoidal

8. What is antrum of Highmore ? Where it opens ?

Ans. Maxillary air sinus is called sinus of Highmore.

It opens in the posterior part of middle meatus of nose.

9. Enumerate the structures in midline of neck.

Ans. Symphysis menti *or* chin

Body of hyoid bone

Thyroid cartilage – Adam's apple

Cricoid cartilage

Tracheal rings

Isthmus on 2nd / 3rd / 4th tracheal rings

Suprasternal notch.

10. What are the subdivisions of anterior triangle of neck ?

Ans. 1. Submental Δ

2. Digastric Δ

3. Carotid Δ

4. Muscular Δ.

11. Name the branches of external carotid artery.

Ans.
1. Superior thyroid artery
2. Lingual artery — From front
3. Facial artery
4. Occipital artery
5. Posterior auricular artery — From back

Terminal — 6. Superficial temporal

Branches — 7. Maxillary artery

From medial side — ascending pharyngeal artery

Total 8 branches

12. What are Infrahyoid muscles and give their nerve supply.

Ans. 1. Sternohyoid

2. Sternothyroid

3. Thyrohyoid

4. Omohyoid

Nerve supply – Ansa cervicalis

13. What is pterion ? Give its surgical importance.

Ans. Pterion is the meeting point of 4 bones:

1. Frontal
2. Parietal
3. Temporal
4. Sphenoid

This union is H-shaped and situated on normal lateralis.

Importance: Lies deep to it — anterior branches of middle meningeal artery. Due to any injury here, it ruptures — causes extradural haematoma.

Other structures are:

1. Middle meningeal vein
2. Stem of lateral sulcus.

14. Enumerate paired dural venous sinuses.

Ans. 1. Cavernous sinus

2. Superior petrosal sinus

3. Inferior petrosal sinus

4. Transverse sinus
5. Sigmoid sinus
6. Sphenoparietal sinus.

15. Enumerate unpaired dural venous sinuses.

Ans. 1. Superior sagittal sinus
2. Inferior sagittal sinus
3. Straight sinus
4. Occipital sinus
5. Anterior intercavernous sinus
6. Posterior intercavernous sinus.

16. Contents of temporal fossa:

Ans. This lies medial to zygomatic arch:

1. Temporalis muscle
2. Deep temporal vessels
3. Deep temporal nerves
4. Auriculotemporal nerve
5. Superficial temporal artery.

17. What are the contents of the infratemporal fossa ?

Ans. 1. Lateral pterygoid muscle
2. Medial pterygoid muscle
3. Mandibular nerve and its branches
4. Otic ganglion
5. Chorda tympani nerve
6. Pterygoid venous plexus.

18. Name the two sites where branches of internal and external carotid artery anastomose.

Ans. Two sites:

1. On the scalp where the superficial temporal and supraorbital artery anastomose
2. At medial angle of eye — branches of facial artery anastomose with branches of ophthalmic artery.

19. Name the paired bones of skull.

Ans.
1. Parietal
2. Temporal
3. Zygomatic
4. Nasal
5. Maxilla
6. Lacrimal
7. Palatine
8. Inferior nasal conchae.

20. Unpaired bones of facial skeleton.

Ans.
a. Vomer
b. Mandible
c. Frontal
d. Occipital
e. Sphenoid.

21. What are fontanelles ? Enumerate. Give functions of fontanelles.

Ans. Membrane filled gaps in foetal skull or neonatal skull are fontanelles.

1. Anterior fontanelle
2. Posterior fontanelle
3. Two anterolateral fontanelle
4. Two posterolateral fontanelle.

Functions:

1. They cause moulding of skull during childbirth
2. They allow the growth of brain.

22. Name the muscles of mastication. Give their nerve supply and development.

Ans. 1. Masseter

2. Temporalis
3. Lateral pterygoid
4. Medial pterygoid

Nerve supply: Mandibular nerve
Branch of trigeminal nerve

Development: 1st arch mesoderm.

23. Name the structures attached to styloid process.

Ans. Two ligaments:

1. Stylomandibular ligament
2. Stylohyoid ligament

Three muscles:

1. Styloglossus
2. Stylohyoid
3. Stylopharyngeus.

24. Name the nuclei of the cerebellum.

Ans. 1. Nucleus dentate
2. Nucleus emboliformis
3. Nucleus fastigi
4. Nucleus globosus.

25. Inferior cerebellar peduncles:

Ans. These are big bundles of white fibres from medulla oblongata to cerebellum. This carries following tracts:

1. Posterior spinocerebellar tract
2. Vestibulocerebellar
3. Olivocerebellar
4. Reticulocerebellar
5. Parolivocerebellar
6. Cuneocerebellar
7. Trigeminocerebellar.

26. Give the development of thyroid.

Ans. Thyroid gland is endodermal in origin.

It grows from median thyroid diverticulum — which grows from foramen caecum of tongue. This diverticulum grows down in front of midline of neck. Soon it bifurcates and these bifid ends proliferate and form lateral lobes of thyroid — the diverticulum disappears.

If it persists, it forms thyroglossal cyst.

This median thyroid diverticulum also called thyroglossal duct.

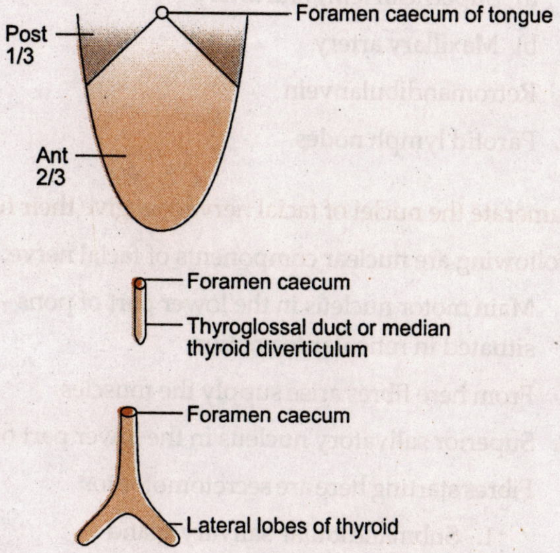

27. What are the derivatives of third pharyngeal pouch ?

Ans. 1. Posterior 1/3 of tongue

2. Thymus

3. Inferior parathyroids.

28. Contents of parotid gland:

Ans. 1. Facial nerve and its 5 terminal branches

a) Temporal

b) Zygomatic

c) Buccal

d) Mandibular

e) Cervical.

2. External carotid artery and its 2 terminal branches

   a) Superficial temporal artery

   b) Maxillary artery

3. Retromandibular vein

4. Parotid lymph nodes.

29. Enumerate the nuclei of facial nerve and give their functions.

Ans. Following are nuclear components of facial nerve:

1. Main motor nucleus in the lower part of pons – deeply situated in reticular formation

   From here fibres arise supply the muscles

2. Superior salivatory nucleus in the lower part of pons

   Fibres starting here are secretomotor to:

   1. Submandibular salivary gland
   2. Sublingual salivary gland

3. Lacrimatory nucleus –

   Through pterygopalatine ganglion fibres are distributed to lacrimal gland

4. Nucleus of tractus solitarius

   It is in medulla oblongata

   Fibres of taste from anterior 2/3 of tongue are received by this nucleus through chorda tympani nerve.

30. Nuclei of trigeminal nerve:

Ans. 1. Main sensory nucleus in the upper part of pons.

2. Medial to above nucleus lies small motor nucleus.

Fibres from this nucleus are distributed to muscles of mastication via the mandibular branch of trigeminal nerve.

3. Mesencephalic nucleus of trigeminal
– lies in the whole length of midbrain.

4. Spinal nucleus of trigeminal — main sensory nucleus extends up to C 1, C 2 part of spinal cord.

31. Enumerate the muscles supplied by oculomotor nerve.

Ans. 1. Levator palpebrae superioris

2. Superior rectus

3. Inferior rectus

4. Medial rectus

5. Inferior oblique

↓

Branch to this muscle joins ciliary ganglion and supplies:

6. Sphincter pupillae

7. Ciliaris muscle.

32. What is secretomotor nerve supply of parotid gland ?

Ans. The secretomotor nerve supply begins in the inferior salivatory nucleus lies in the lower part of pons.

Fibres taken by lesser petrosal of glossopharyngeal nerve to otic ganglion.

In the otic ganglion — relay.

Postganglionic fibres taken by the auriculotemporal nerve to parotid gland.

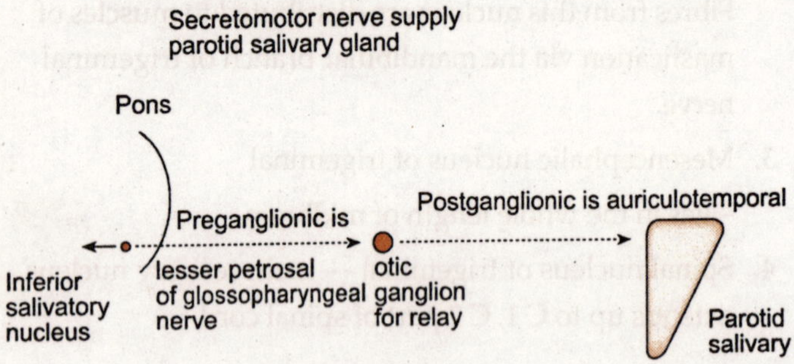

33. Secretomotor nerve supply to:
    1. Submandibular salivary gland
    2. Sublingual salivary gland.

Ans.

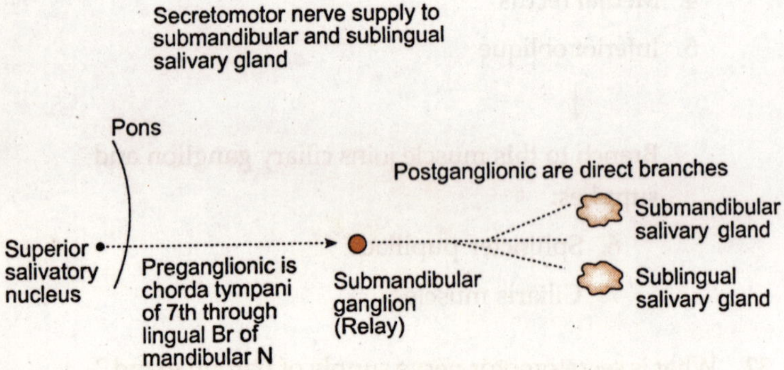

The secretomotor nerve supply starts at superior salivatory nucleus lies in the lower part of pons fibres taken to submandibular ganglion, here relay take place.

Postganglionic are distal branches go to:

1. Submandibular salivary gland
2. Sublingual salivary gland.

34. Name the muscles supplied by mandibular nerve.

Ans. 1. Masseter
2. Temporalis
3. Lateral pterygoid
4. Medial pterygoid
5. Mylohyoid
6. Anterior belly of Digastric muscle
7. Tensor tympani
8. Tensor palati.

35. Name the cartilages of larynx.

Ans. 3 unpaired – thyroid cartilage
– cricoid cartilage
– epiglottis

3 paired – arytenoid
– corniculate
– cuneiform (total nine cartilages).

36. OINA of Cricothyroid muscle:

Ans. Cricothyroid is the intrinsic muscle of larynx which lies outside the larynx.

O – Cricoid cartilage

I – Thyroid cartilage

NS – Superior laryngeal nerve — branch of vagus nerve

A – Tenses the vocal cords
+
Increases pitch of voice

37. Nerve supply of posterior belly of Digastric muscle and its embryological reason.

Ans. Postbelly of Digastric muscle develops from 2nd arch mesoderm, so supplied by the nerve of 2nd arch, i.e. facial nerve.

38. Function of Orbicularis oculi muscle:

Ans. This is the muscle of face around eye called sphincter of eye, hence does closure of eye — light, as during sleep

+

blinking tight — as we want to avoid sun rays, wind, etc.

Thus prevents dryness of cornea, give the protection to eye by doing closure of eye.

Blinking — called involuntary contractions, spread the lacrimal fluid over whole eye and thus eye is kept moist and clean.

39. Nasal septum:

Ans. Formed by:

1. Perpendicular plate of ethmoid
2. Vomer
3. Septal cartilage
4. Skin.

40. Give the development of pituitary gland.

Ans. Pituitary gland has 2 parts —

1. Large anterior part called adenohypophysis

2. Small posterior part called neurohypophysis

Adenohypophysis develops from Rathke's pouch — ectodermal

Diverticulum grows up from stomodeum — from growing mouth

Neurohypophysis — from neuroectoderm grows from floor of third ventricle.

41. Explain confluence of sinuses.

Ans. This is the posterior dilated end of the sagittal sinus — lies slightly right to internal occipital protuberance. At this site 4 sinuses are meeting –

1. End of superior sagittal sinus
2. End of straight sinus
3. Beginning of right transverse sinus
4. Beginning of left transverse sinus.

42. Note on falx cerebri.

Ans. – Sickle-shaped double fold of dura mater

– Attached anter orly to crista galli and posteriorly, no bony attachment

– In its superior margin lies superior sagittal sinus

– In its inferior border lies the inferior sagittal sinus

– Stem of the sickle contains straight sinus

Function:

1. 2 layers enclose the venous blood called dural sinuses

2. Stabilises the brain in the cranial cavity, so does not allow the movement of brain even if so many jerks are felt on the skull.

Diagram of falx cerebri

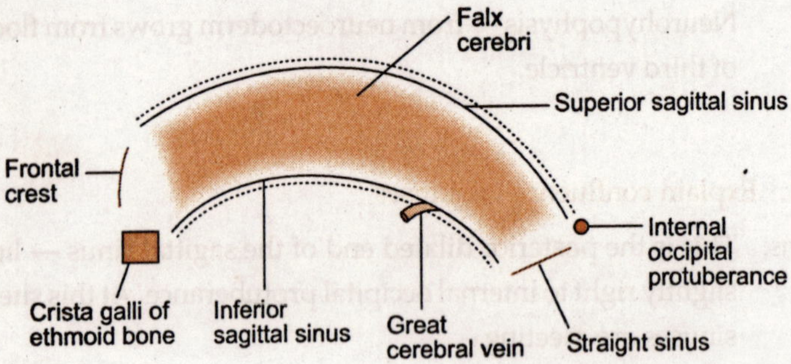

Multiple Choice Questions

1) Spinal cord is made up of:
   a. Thirty segments
   b. Thirty one segments
   c. Thirty two segments
   d. Thirty three segments

2) Ligamentum denticulatum is formed by:
   a. Pia mater
   b. Gray matter
   c. Arachnoid mater
   d. Dura mater

3) Number of pairs of cervical nerves attached to spinal cord:
   a. Five
   b. Six
   c. Seven
   d. Eight

4) Posterior funiculus contains:
   a. Fasciculus gracilis
   b. Fasciculus cuneatus
   c. a + b
   d. Spinothalamic tract

5) In central nervous system myelin sheaths are formed by:
   a. Schwann cells
   b. Oligodendrocytes
   c. Astrocytes
   d. Ependymal cells

Ans. 1. b 2. a 3. d 4. c 5. b

6) Parasympathetic nucleus of oculomotor is called:
   a. Nucleus ambiguous
   b. Edinger Westphal nucleus
   c. Superior salivatory nucleus
   d. Nucleus of tractus solitarius

7) Nucleus of tractus solitarius is concerned with:
   a. Smell sensation b. Taste sensation
   c. Touch sensation d. Pain sensation

8) Arcuate nuclei are:
   a. Neurones of pontine nuclei
   b. Neurones of inferior olivary nucleus
   c. Neurones of auditory pathway
   d. None of the above

9) Motor nucleus of trigeminal nerve lies in:
   a. Upper part of pons b. Lower part of pons
   c. Midbrain d. Medulla oblongata

10) Connection of pons with cerebellum is through:
   a. Superior cerebellar peduncles
   b. Middle cerebellar peduncles
   c. Inferior cerebellar peduncles
   d. None of the above

Ans. 6. b 7. b 8. a 9. a 10. b

11) Example of neurobiotaxis is:

a. Facial colliculus b. Superior colliculus

c. Inferior colliculus d. None of the above

12) Trapezoid body is present in:

a. Midbrain b. Pons

c. Cerebellum d. Medulla

13) Following parts are having visual function:

a. Superior colliculus of midbrain

b. Lateral geniculate body

c. Retrolentiform part of internal capsule

d. All of the above

14) Medial geniculate bodies receive afferents from:

a. Superior colliculus b. Inferior colliculus

c. Pons d. Medulla oblongata

15) Maintenance of equilibrium is the function of:

a. Neocerebellum b. Corpus striatum

c. Paleocerebellum d. Archecerebellum

16) Following are nuclei of cerebellum *except*:

a. Dentate nucleus b. Olivary nucleus

c. Emboliformis nucleus d. Fastigi nucleus

Ans. 11. a 12. b 13. d 14. b 15. d 16. b

17) Anterior spinocerebellar tract passes through:

a. Inferior cerebellar peduncles

b. Middle cerebellar peduncles

c. Superior cerebellar peduncles

d. Cerebral peduncles

18) Cerebral aqueduct has following features *except*:

a. Occupies whole length of midbrain

b. Lined by ependyma

c. Connects two lateral ventricles

d. Connects third ventricle with fourth ventricle

19) Main pathway of middle cerebellar peduncle is:

a. Anterior spinocerebellar

b. Olivocerebellar

c. Cortico-ponto-cerebellar

d. Vestibulocerebellar

20) Fibres connecting two cerebral hemispheres are:

a. Commissural fibres b. Association fibres

c. Arcuate fibres d. Projection fibres

21) Foramen of Monro connects:

a. Third ventricle with fourth ventricle

b. Two lateral ventricles

c. Fourth ventricle with subarachnoid space

d. Fourth ventricle with central canal of spinal cord

Ans. 17. c 18. d 19. c 20. a 21. b

22) Following fibres are commissural fibres:

a. Internal capsule
b. Corpus callosum
c. Fornix
d. b + c

23) Broca's area is on:

a. Superior temporal gyrus
b. Superior frontal gyrus
c. Inferior frontal gyrus
d. Middle frontal gyrus

24) Cingulum is the example of:

a. Association fibres
b. Commissural fibres
c. Projection fibres
d. None of the above

25) Uncus is associated with the function of:

a. Taste
b. Smell
c. Vision
d. Hearing

26) Optic radiation fibres pass through:

a. Anterior limb of internal capsule
b. Sublentiform part of internal capsule
c. Retrolentiform part of internal capsule
d. None of the above

Ans. 22. d 23. c 24. a 25. b 26. c

27) Forceps minor fibres of corpus callosum connects:

a. Two frontal lobes

b. Two parietal lobes

c. Two temporal lobes

d. Two occipital lobes

28) Corpus callosum connects following two lobes *except*:

a. Parietal lobes
b. Temporal lobes
c. Occipital lobes
d. Frontal lobes

29) Following are examples of projection fibres *except*:

a. Corona radiata
b. Pyramidal tract
c. External capsule
d. Internal capsule

30) Through sublentiform part of internal capsule passes:

a. Optic radiation fibres

b. Auditory radiation fibres

c. Corona radiata

d. None of the above

31) Extent of spinal cord is from:

a. Foramen magnum to sacral second vertebra

b. Foramen magnum to lower border of first lumbar vertebra

c. Atlas to lower border of first lumbar vertebra

d. Atlas to second sacral vertebra

Ans. 27. a 28. b 29. c 30. b 31. c

32) In-co-ordination of movements are due to:

a. Cerebral disease

b. Cerebellum dysfunction

c. Brainstem lesion

d. None of the above

33) Cerebrospinal fluid is formed by:

a. Arachnoid granulation

b. Dura mater sinuses

c. Choroid plexus

d. None of the above

34) Following nerves are purely sensory:

a. Olfactory b. Optic

c. Vestibulocochlear d. All of the above

35) Pain temperature pathway is:

a. Spinocerebellar tract

b. Anterior spinothalamic tract

c. Lateral spinothalamic tract

d. None of the above

36) The pyramidal decussation takes place in:

a. Upper part of medulla oblongata

b. Lower part of medulla oblongata

c. Middle medulla

d. Lower part of pons

Ans. 32. b 33. c 34. d 35. c 36. b

37) Following nucleus lies in midbrain:

a. Red nucleus

b. Inferior olivary nucleus

c. Superior salivatory nucleus

d. Inferior salivatory nucleus

38) Central sulcus is called:

a. Operculated sulcus

b. Limiting sulcus

c. a + b

d. Complete sulcus

39) Filum terminale is continuation of:

a. Pia mater b. Dura mater

c. Arachnoid mater d. Gray matter

40) Subarachnoid space contains:

a. Blood vessels which supply the brain

b. Cerebrospinal fluid

c. a + b

d. Arachnoid granulations

Ans. 37. a 38. b 39. a 40. c

Short Answer Questions

1. Name the different parts of lateral ventricle.

Ans. Central part lies in parietal lobe.

Anterior horn lies in frontal lobe.

Posterior horn lies in occipital lobe.

Inferior horn lies in temporal lobe.

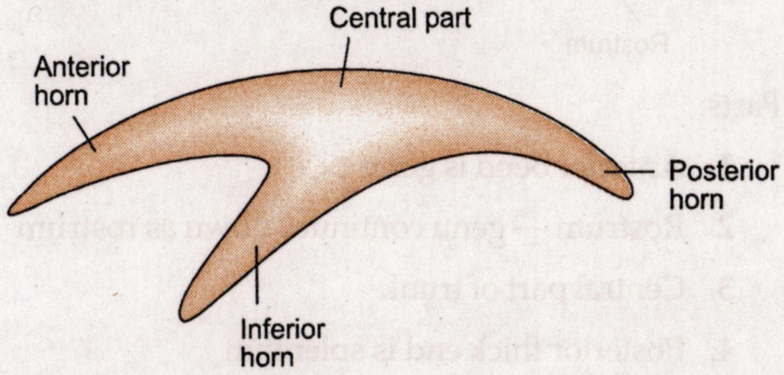

2. Name the types of white fibres of cerebrum.

Ans. 1. Association fibres

2. Projection fibres

3. Commissural fibres

3. Name the different commissural fibres of cerebrum.

Ans. 1. Corpus callosum

2. Anterior commissure

3. Posterior commissure

4. Fornix

5. Hippocampal commissure

4. What are different parts of corpus callosum ? Draw diagram.

Ans.

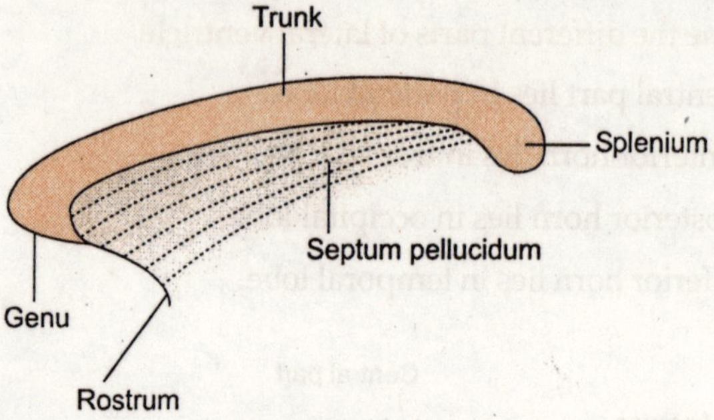

Parts:

1. Anterior bend is genu
2. Rostrum — genu continues down as rostrum
3. Central part of trunk
4. Posterior thick end is splenium

5. Define third ventricle. What are recesses of third ventricle ?

Ans. Median slit-like cavity of diencephalon is third ventricle. It lies in between two thalami. Recesses are:

1. Optic
2. Supraoptic
3. Pineal
4. Infundibular

6. Enumerate the structures in the floor of third ventricle.

Ans.
1. Optic chiasma
2. Tuber cinereum
3. Infundibulum
4. Mammillary bodies
5. Posterior perforated substance
6. Tegmentum of midbrain

7. What is internal capsule ? What are parts of internal capsule?

Ans. Internal capsule is an example of projection fibres.

Parts:

1. Anterior limb
2. Genu
3. Posterior limb
4. Retrolentiform part
5. Sublentiform part

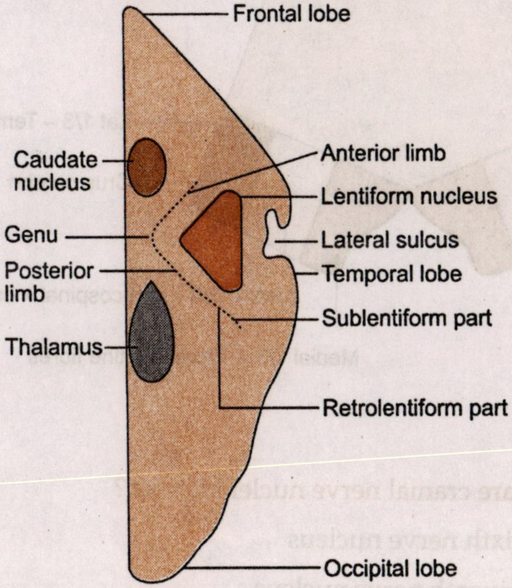

8. What are basal nuclei of cerebrum ?

Ans. a. Corpus striatum — made up of:

1. Caudate nucleus 2. Lentiform nucleus

b. Claustrum

c. Amygdaloid body

9. What are the fibres in crus cerebri of midbrain ?

Ans. 1. Middle 2/3rd — corticospinal or pyramidal tract

2. Medial 1/3rd — frontopontine fibres

3. Lateral 1/3rd — temporopontine fibres

T.S. of midbrain shows above fibres.

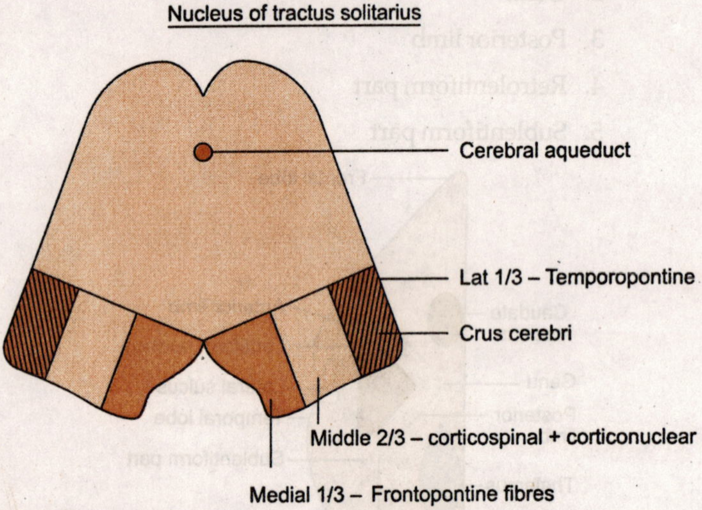

10. What are cranial nerve nuclei in pons ?

Ans. 1. Sixth nerve nucleus

2. Seventh nerve nucleus

3. Fifth nerve nucleus

4. Vestibular nuclei of 8th nerve

5. Cochlear nuclei of 8th nerve

6. Superior and inferior salivatory nuclei.

11. Medial longitudinal bundle:

Ans. Nuclei of 3rd, 4th, 5th, 6th and 11th cranial nerve are connected by this bundle.

— This is called association tract.

12. Give the functional classification of cerebellum.

Ans.
1. Archicerebellum — oldest part maintains equilibrium
2. Paleocerebellum — maintains tone and posture and crude movements of limb
3. Neocerebellum — co-ordinates and controls fine movements of body.

13. Gray matter masses of cerebellum:

Ans.
1. Nucleus dentatus
2. Nucleus globosus
3. Nucleus emboliformis
4. Nucleus fastigi.

14. Inferior cerebellar peduncle:

Ans. Bundle of white fibres from medulla oblongata:

1. Cerebellovestibular + vestibulocerebellar
2. Cerebelloolivary and olivocerebellar
3. Cerebelloreticular and reticulocerebellar
4. Olivocerebellar
5. Posterior spinocerebellar
6. Cuneocerebellar
7. Trigeminocerebellar
8. Anterior external arcuate fibres to cerebellum

15. Cranial nerve nuclei in the floor of fourth ventricle:

Ans. 1. Hypoglossal nucleus

2. Dorsal nucleus of vagus

3. Sixth nerve nucleus

4. Vestibular nuclei

5. Nucleus of tractus solitarius.

16. Ciliary ganglion:

Ans. This is peripheral parasympathetic ganglion on the course of oculomotor nerve.

It is near apex of orbit connections.

1. Motor root — nerve to Inferior oblique
2. Sensory root — form nasociliary nerve
3. Sympathetic root — a branch from plexus around internal carotid artery.

Branches:

8–10 branches supply

1. Ciliaris
2. Sphincter pupillae.

17. What are effects of injury to oculomotor nerve ?

Ans. 1. Paralysis of Levator palpebrae superioris leads to ptosis – i.e. drooping of upper eyelid

2. Squint due to paralysis of:

– Superior rectus

– Medial rectus

– Inferior rectus

3. Dilatation of pupil — paralysis of Sphincter pupillae
4. Loss of accommodation due to paralysis of Ciliaris.

18. What is nucleus ambiguous ?

Ans. This is motor nucleus.

It is complex nucleus which lies in medulla oblongata.

It is elongated column of gray matter representing three nerves: 9th, 10th, 11th.

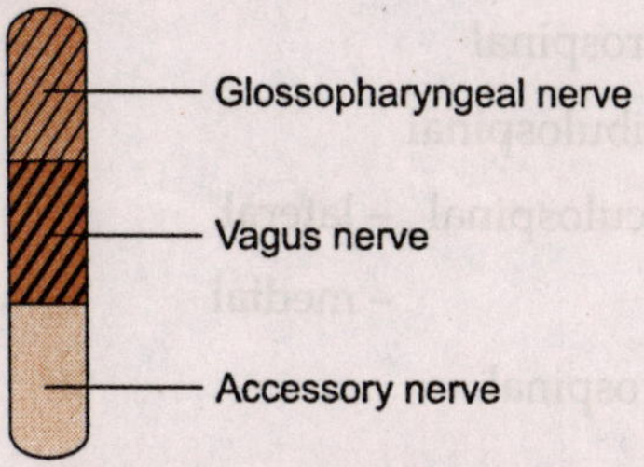

19. What is nucleus of tractus solitarius ?

Ans. – This is special sensory nucleus receiving the taste fibres from tongue

– Elongated column of gray matter in medulla oblongata represent three nerves: 7th, 9th, 10th.

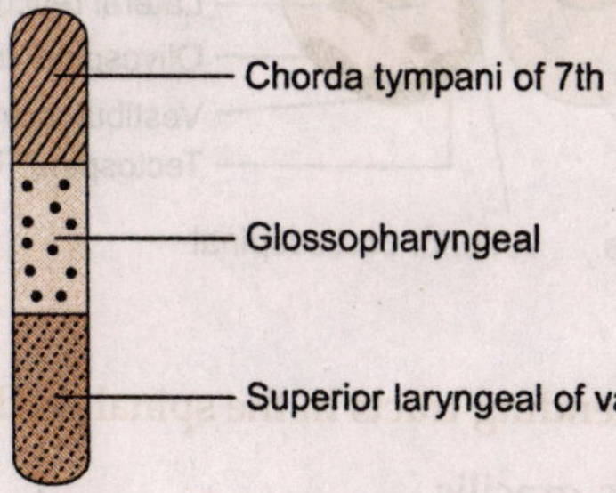

20. Enumerate descending tracts in spinal cord.

Ans. Pyramidal tract – Crossed pyramidal

or

– Lateral corticospinal uncrossed pyramides of anterior corticospinal tracts

Extrapyramidal

1. Tectospinal
2. Rubrospinal
3. Vestibulospinal
4. Reticulospinal – lateral
   – medial
5. Olivospinal.

Descending tracts in TS of spinal cord

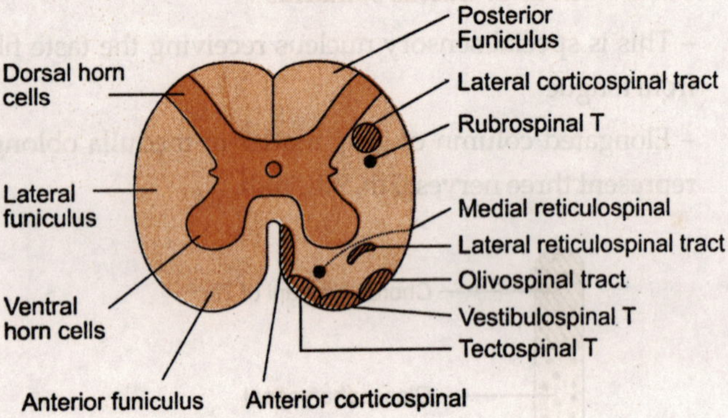

21. Enumerate ascending tracts in the spinal cord.

Ans. 1. Fasciculus gracilis

2. Fasciculus cuneatus

3. Lateral spinothalamic tract
4. Anterior spinothalamic tract
5. Anterior spinocerebellar
6. Posterior spinocerebellar.

Ascending tracts in TS spinal cord

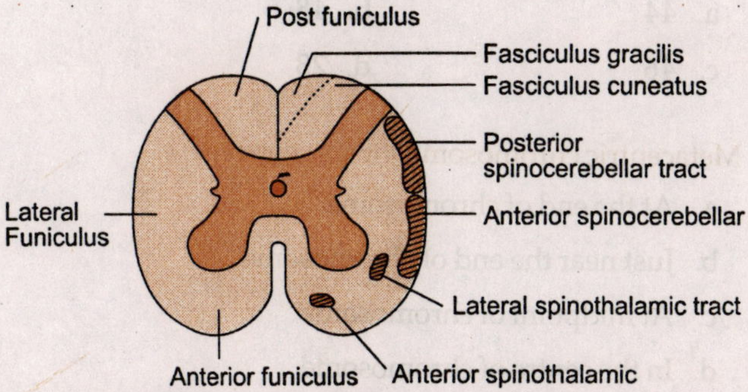

22. Enumerate different types of sulci of cerebrum giving one example of each.

Ans. 1. Limiting sulcus — central sulcus
2. Axial sulcus — postcalcarine sulcus
3. Operculated sulcus — lunate sulcus
4. Secondary sulcus — lateral sulcus
   – parietooccipital
5. Complete sulcus — collateral
   – precalcarine.

Chapter 10: Genetics

Multiple Choice Questions

1) No. of chromosomes in human beings:

   a. 44 b. 48

   c. 46 d. 23

2) Metacentric chromosome shows centromere:

   a. At the end of chromosome

   b. Just near the end of chromosome

   c. At midpoint of chromosome

   d. In the centre of chromosome

3) The telocentric chromosome shows centromere:

   a. At the end of chromosome

   b. In the centre

   c. Slightly away from midpoint

   d. None of the above

4) Barr body is:

   a. Inactive Y chromosome

   b. Inactive X chromosome

   c. Autosome

   d. None of the above

Ans. 1. c 2. d 3. a 4. b

5) Loss of some portion of chromosome is:

a. Deletion b. Insertion

c. Inversion d. Translocation

6) Down syndrome is:

a. Trisomy 13 b. Trisomy 21

c. Trisomy 18 d. Trisomy 10

7) Webbed neck is in:

a. Turner's syndrome

b. Down's syndrome

c. Klinefelter's syndrome

d. None of the above

8) 47xxy is:

a. Down's syndrome b. Klinefelter's syndrome

c. a + b d. Turner's syndrome

9) X-linked gene is always explained in:

a. Males b. Females

c. Both the sexes d. None of the above

10) Hairy ear pinna is example of:

a. Autosomal inheritance

b. X-linked inheritance

c. Y-linked inheritance

d. None of the above

Ans. 5. a 6. b 7. a 8. b 9. a 10. c

11) Haemophilia is the example of:

a. Autosomal dominant inheritance

b. Autosomal recessive inheritance

c. X-linked recessive inheritance

d. X-linked dominant inheritance

12) XYY is also called:

a. Mongolism
b. Supermale
c. Down's syndrome
d. Turner syndrome

13) Reduction of chromosome number from diploid to haploid in:

a. Mitosis
b. Meiosis
c. Both of the above
d. None of the above

14) At which cell stage of cell division in mitosis chromosomal study done for karyotyping?

a. Anaphase
b. Prophase
c. Metaphase
d. Telophase

15) Colour blindness is:

a. Autosomal recessive inheritance

b. X-linked recessive inheritance

c. Autosomal dominant inheritance

d. None of the above

Ans. 11. c 12. b 13. b 14. c 15. b

Short Answer Questions

1. Turner's syndrome:

Ans. 1. Person is of short stature
2. Webbing of neck
3. Wide chest
4. Poorly developed breasts
5. Primary amenorrhoea
6. No proper growth of external genitalia
7. No proper growth of female reproductive organs

2. Klinefelter's syndrome:

Ans. 1. Persons are tall
2. Gynecomastia — growth of breasts in males
3. Small testes — seminiferous tubules not showing spermatogenic cells
4. Poor development of secondary sexual characters.

3. Down's syndrome:

Ans. 1. Person is mentally retarded
2. Oblique palpebral fissure
3. Brachycephaly
4. Low bridge of nose
5. Tongue shows furrows and it is protruding
6. Short stature.

4. What is Barr body ?

Ans. 1. It is called sex chromatin

2. It is small chromatin body detected in the interphase of female mammals

3. It is stained by basic dyes

4. Barr body is derived from one of the X chromosomes which is condensed and inactive.

5. Enumerate structural chromosomal aberrations.

Ans. 1. Deletion

2. Duplication

3. Translocation

4. Inversion

5. Ring chromosome.

6. Classify chromosomes:

Ans. 1. Metacentric

2. Submetacentric

3. Telocentric

4. Acrocentric.

7. What is gene ? Give the functions of gene.

Ans. DNA molecule is gene.

It is responsible for transmission of hereditary factors to next generation.

Functions are:

1. Formation of RNA

2. Genes regulate protein synthesis

3. Regulates the activity of other genes
4. Regulates mitosis
5. Regulates cell growth
6. Also helps in differentiation of cells embryologically.

8. What are cases where genetic counselling is needed ?

Ans. 1. Recurrent abortions
2. Child abortions
3. Infertility
4. Prenatal diagnosis for late maternal age
5. Risk of recurrence of a hereditary disease in family.

9. What are the indications for prenatal diagnosis ?

Ans. 1. Pregnancy in late age of the woman
2. Having a previous child with some chromosomal abnormality
3. If chromosomal abnormality is detected in one of the parents
4. If there is family history of some genetic defect and by DNA study such defect is anticipated
5. If there is any risk of neural tube defect.

10. What are most commonly used cells in karyotyping ?

Ans. 1. Fibroblasts in the deeper part of skin
2. Bone marrow cells
3. Peripheral blood cells
4. Cells in amniotic fluid.

11. Define:
    1. Genotype
    2. Phenotype.

Ans. Genotype of the individual is the genetic constitution of the individual.

Phenotype is expression of any of the genes as physical, biochemical or physiological trail.

12. Give the definition of mutation. Give the causes of mutation.

Ans. Mutation is any sudden heritable change in DNA in which gene undergoes a structural change.

Causes: 1. Spontaneous

2. Some exogenous agents are responsible

Example – ionising radiations

– chemicals like mustard gas

– some viruses.